Living in Rome

LIVING IN ROME

a 9/11 story

HOMER VAN METER

Mach 10 Publishing

Rhinelander, Wisconsin

LIVING IN ROME. Copyright © 2020 by Homer Van Meter. All rights reserved. No part of this publication may be reproduced, stored or transmitted in any form or by any means, electronic, mechanical, photocopying, recording, scanning, or otherwise without written permission from the publisher. It is illegal to copy this book, post it to a website, or distribute it by any other means without permission.

Published in the United States of America by Mach10 Publishing.

Photograph credits:

Page 198 © Darlene Machtan.

Cover – Majestic United States Flag against a dark background © ungvar/Shutterstock.com.

ISBN 978-1-7344758-3-8 (pbk)

ISBN 978-1-7344758-2-1 (ebook)

Printed in the United States of America

Book design by Nan Andrews

2 4 6 8 10 9 7 5 3 1

First edition: March 2020

CONTENTS

Other books by Homer Van Meter	vii
Dedication	1
Chapter One	3
Chapter Two	23
Chapter Three	38
Chapter Four	83
Chapter Five	111
Chapter Six	156
Chapter Seven	164
Chapter Eight	186
Epilogue	191
About the Author	197

OTHER BOOKS BY HOMER VAN METER

Day of the Little Guy
4900 Nights: A True Story of Reincarnation
The Dreaming Time: Anatomy of a Cover-Up

Mach10 Publishing

DEDICATION

To
Cyril Hynes
who truly is a remarkable character
and
Ed Novak
for making the most accurate
prediction of evil that history has yet seen

CHAPTER ONE

There are only three things in our lives which we have absolutely no control of: the particular genetic makeup which we are granted, and the time and place where we are born. Beyond our infancy in those inherited circumstances, we are all participants to some infinitesimal degree in all which transpires in the world around us. Responsibility ever weighs on the few who realize this, while ignorance constantly crushes and rules the masses who deny this truth. Life is measured by defining moments, both large and small, and it is how we influence, and are influenced by them, which speaks of our character.

When one looks past the overbearing, sweeping generalizations of history, what remains are the stories of those directly affected by the events of the times. The popular accounts are often false narratives, contrived to promote an agenda, while the experiences of individuals caught in the middle of the fray are very real and true.

For those of us who were alive in September of

the year 2001, there came a very defining moment. For a few days in the middle of that tragic month, I knew a man named Tom Coach. He seemed like an ordinary enough guy at first glance, but by the time our brief acquaintance had concluded, I knew I had born witness to the trials of a man thrust into the midst of an awful moment in history.

It was three o'clock when the bell rang at the end of his last class that Friday afternoon. Tom crammed his lecture notes into his briefcase and stood looking around, almost wistfully, as his students collected themselves and filed out of the lecture hall. He grabbed the briefcase and followed the last one out the door. Dodging students, who were always in more of a hurry than he was, he made his way down the hall and up the stairs to his office.

He stood bent over behind his desk in the little, square office for a couple minutes, arranging papers and filing things away, until he was satisfied that he could leave things as they were and make his escape. Reaching for the daily calendar on the corner of his desk, he tore the page with that day's date off of it, crumpled it up and dropped it into the waste basket. In his mind, Friday, September seven, 2001 had just concluded. He stood upright, took a quick scan of the office and announced to himself, "I'm outta here."

Leaving everything in the office except his jacket, he stepped out into the hallway and locked the door behind him. He straightened up and was just starting down the hall, when one of his colleagues came past and walked with him.

"No briefcase going home with the professor this weekend?"

"That's right," Tom said. "No papers, no reports, no nothing – for the next nine days, I'm going to pretend that this place does not exist."

"Now I remember. You're off next week."

"You remember you're covering one of my comp classes, right?" Tom asked, glancing sideways at the man as they turned and started down the stairs.

"Sure, oh sure. At least I would have remembered when I looked at the calendar on Monday."

"That's reassuring," Tom said.

They turned and went down another flight of stairs and then started down the hallway on the ground floor.

"So, how by the grace of the all-mighty did you manage to get a week off in September?" The friend asked.

"The privilege of tenure," Tom replied, facetiously. "After twenty years in this place, they conceded to let me teach eight weeks of summer school for the past two years and do an infinite amount of groveling for this measly week off."

"Oh, the privileges," his friend, Al, commiserated.

They turned a corner and continued on their way to the exit.

"I've forgotten. Where is it that you are going on this privileged vacation?" Al asked.

"Newfoundland – moose hunting."

The man lifted his eyebrows as they clopped down the hall.

"I gather you're not talking about taking pictures?"

Only in New York, Tom thought. Only in New York City would a man hear a comment like that.

"How perceptive you are," Tom replied. "No, I'm not going to Newfoundland to merely take pictures. I'm going to tramp out into the wilderness with a rifle and gun down a magnificent, defenseless creature in cold blood. Next week is going to be about blood and guts – real cold, calculated premeditated, carnage."

"I just love it when you talk dirty like that," Al responded in a lilting, kidding voice. "So, what do you do with this moose after you shoot him?"

Tom liked his colleague very much, but he sometimes pitied him for being a native New Yorker.

"I'm going to eat him," he replied.

They were approaching the big doors at the front of the building.

"What if they call you up this evening and say they can't find enough people to cover your classes?"

"You worry too much, Al," Tom said. "For me, it's clear and simple. I've had this trip planned for almost two years. When I step through that door, I'm gone. Next week, it's your baby."

They stepped through the doors and out into the sunshine. Tom veered away from Al and quickened his pace. He glanced at his watch. He was taking an earlier train than usual. If he hurried, he thought, he could just make it.

It was a pleasant afternoon outside. Tom normally wasn't in this much of a hurry as he walked down the street on such afternoons. The university was almost an artificial, separate world in the middle of the city and he didn't mind taking the time to enjoy it. However, today he had things to do.

The street was full of people, mostly college students. Some were standing around, or sitting on steps conversing in their own little cliques. Mostly though, they were like Tom, charging off to somewhere. It was Friday. Things were happening or would be happening that evening. Everyone, it seemed, had somewhere to get to or something to prepare for.

A pair of college students stood at the railing where the stairs descended to the subway. The guy was dressed in khaki pants with a camouflage knapsack over one shoulder. The girl was lean with waist length, honey colored hair and a long skirt that looked like a giant red bandana. By their appearance, if they weren't in love, they soon would be – or at least pretending to be for the weekend. Tom stepped past them and rushed down the stairs. He took the jacket from where he had been carrying it over his shoulder, reached into the pocket and retrieved a token, which he methodically plunked into the slot at the turnstyle. He walked very fast out onto the platform. The train came pulling in and the doors opened. Tom never broke stride until he had stepped into a car. Just barely made it, he thought. The doors slammed shut and the train went speeding off.

It was only then that Tom looked around him as he stood in the car, hanging onto the pipe just above his head. One could never be entirely sure just what he was stepping into when he got into a subway car. It was often the same when one stepped back out onto a platform. With one short step, across a small threshold, one could leave a relatively safe environment and enter a violent, hostile one. It was an unpredictable reality, and it was the story of New York. Tom, himself, had once been beaten by a trio of thugs and robbed on a subway platform. He had sworn then to be more careful, but there was a limit to how much caution one could exercise and still function in the city.

In places, it seemed to be a city of splendor, an affirmative repository of all which was cultured and refined in the human world. However, one frequently needed only to travel a couple blocks from such a sphere of radiant, ethereal grace to find he was in the armpit of the universe. Sadly, there seemed to be little reconciliation between the two extremes, and it seemed that the former was in a constant struggle to remain elevated above the latter.

At the next station the train pulled into, a middle-aged man in a slightly shoddy, dark blue polyester suit stood at the edge of the platform urinating over the side, onto the tracks. A few yards away, a ragged bum who, by all appearances, had no intention of ever getting on a train, sat on the concrete with his back against a pillar and his legs extended straight out in front of him. As the doors opened, a woman and her young daughter exited the car past the man in the blue suit with his penis in his hand. The man nonchalantly stepped into the car, gave his dick a shake, tucked it back into his trousers and zipped up. Tom gave the man a wary look. The man merely glanced at him, gave out a gravelly cough and slumped into the seat which had just been vacated by the woman.

The train went speeding off again. Tom looked down at the drunk slumped into the seat. The man wasn't much older than he was. Like most other such people whom he encountered on a daily basis in his comings and goings, he didn't even want to guess what his story was. There were too many stories like that in New York and the only way the average person could function was to ignore them and move on. The woman and the girl who had left the car at the last station could just as well have been Tom's wife and daughter. His wife, Barbara, was a native New Yorker. She had, no doubt, brushed past guys like this drunk, and worse, a thousand times or more in her life. Everyday occurrences such as this got brushed off and never thought about again in New York. At what point in the past, Tom wondered, did society step across the threshold which allowed such behavior to become so common.

A few minutes later, Tom was off the train and walking down the street toward home. He ducked into a small, neighborhood grocery store to buy a loaf of fresh garlic bread and a bottle of wine for dinner. He had been in the place dozens of times over the years. It was usually a fairly quiet, peaceful shop, patronized by local people who were usually fairly civil.

There was a man checking out at the counter. He was probably thirty years old, dressed in typical casual clothes. At a glance, he looked like just an ordinary guy, going on his ordinary way, buying a few groceries. He handed his money to the clerk and she handed him back his change. The man picked up the coins from the counter and examined them in his hand.

"You shorted me a dime," he said to the clerk.

"What?" she asked.

He held out his hand to show her the coins.

"You shorted me a dime. It was eighteen thirty-four. You gave me a dollar, two quarters, a nickel and a penny for change from a twenty."

The man was clearly annoyed. The young woman looked at him from across the counter very attentively.

"You shorted me a dime," the man said again very insistently.

"I'm sorry," the clerk said. She pulled a dime out of

the cash register and handed it to the man. The man pocketed the change, picked up his bag of groceries and turned toward the door.

"Stupid bitch," he said, as he stepped away and went out the door.

The young woman was shaking off the insult as Tom stepped up and set his items on the counter. He looked after the man going out the door. He wondered if there was anywhere left in America, out there in the vast rural reaches, where a John Wayne character would grab a rude bastard like that, get him in a hammer lock, smack his face against the counter a couple times and make him apologize to a woman for such a remark.

Tom was walking down the sidewalk, approaching his apartment building, when he finally saw something he wanted to see. Two fifth-grade boys were walking along with their backpacks, on their way home from school. One of them was Tom's son. He walked faster to catch up to the two boys.

'Hi guys," he said as he strode up beside the boys.

"Hi Dad," his son, Jeffrey, replied.

It wasn't often Tom came home this early. Running into his son, by chance, was a pleasant treat.

He had apparently interrupted the boy's conversation about something or other, so they walked along in awkward silence. When they stepped through the door into the apartment building, Jeffrey asked, "Dad can I go to Jason's for a while?"

Tom looked down at his son. He knew the two boys frequently played together after school.

"Sure, but not too long. Be home before supper."

The two boys went off running down the hall towards the first floor apartment where Jason lived.

"No running in the hall," Tom called after them. They slowed to a walk and Tom smiled.

He climbed the stairs to the third floor, walked down the hall and unlocked the door to his own apartment. It occurred to him as he stepped inside how he used to feel when he was a kid in Vermont coming home from school at this time of year in the evening. The entire community had seemed like a friendly and safe place. When he had walked across the small town on his way home, he knew most of the people he encountered and they knew him. There was a comfort in that. Even when he was in college and came home on holidays, when he got within ten miles of home he got the warm feeling of being on familiar turf again. He didn't get any of those feelings now until he was inside this building and he didn't completely feel at home until he stepped through the door of this apartment. Everything was much smaller in the city – so many people with so many lives of their own, lived in their own little spaces. New York was a vast network of a gazillion insular units compressed into a concrete maze less than twenty miles wide, which comprised the known world to most of its inhabitants.

Tom spent most of the next two hours dragging

things out and packing for his trip. Clothes, boots, gear he hadn't used for twenty years, and some things, such as the binoculars he had bought only last week, all came out of hiding and fought for a place of their own in the two bags he was taking along. When he finally had the bags stuffed to his satisfaction, he went back out to the kitchen.

His daughter, Jennifer, had come home and was engaged with that favorite pastime of thirteen year old girls, which was gossiping with her friends on the telephone. Tom smiled at her as he stepped past and into the kitchen. He was cooking supper. It was not something he did often, but his wife would not be home in time to do it, and he wanted to have his family together for the meal that evening.

It was 6:30. Jennifer hung up the phone and Tom gave her that imposing, parental look which reminded her that homework was more important than gossip. She went off to her room to get to work. Tom unwrapped the hamburger and dumped it into a cast iron skillet to begin making the spaghetti sauce.

His children were off in their separate rooms doing their homework. Though they were not in his immediate company, he was comforted in a great many ways by their presence. He loved his family. He thought about where his wife was at that moment. He thought it most likely that she was either getting ready to leave the office, or was already on the train coming home. She worked for an investment company, which she had come to own a piece of. In recent years, she made four or five times what he did teaching at the university. Far from being threatened in any way by his wife's success, Tom appreciated her contribution to the family's well-being. The stress level, however, from her long hours of devotion to her business was difficult to manage. Eight years ago, when she had gone back to work full time, after a five year leave with her children, she had taken on more responsibility and begun to make serious money. Tom had been very supportive of her efforts and took more responsibility for the children to accommodate her ever more harrying schedule. Their financial security was no longer in doubt, however, and now he was beginning to question the need for such a frenzied level of devotion to the gathering of wealth. She was caught in a whirlwind of her own making though, and it would not be easy for her to escape it. Nothing Tom said would seriously influence her either. She had always had a strong will, but now she had grown into an executive who asked for his opinion less and less.

At 7:25 the supper was ready. Tom began to wonder if he shouldn't go ahead and feed the children. It would stay warm a little longer without being ruined, he thought, so he decided to wait for his wife a few minutes more.

At 7:30, he yelled, "All right, we're going to eat now."

Just then, the door opened and in stepped his wife. She would have walked right in normally, and dumped her things on the nearest chair. But she was caught by Tom's warm gaze and hesitated, looking back at him. He stepped over to her and gave her a big hug.

"You're the best thing I've seen since this morning," he said.

"Same here," she replied.

Tom took her coat, briefcase and purse and piled them in a chair. Barbara grabbed Jeffrey as the boy stepped into the kitchen and gave him a warm hug.

"Hi, Mom," Jeffrey said, hugging her back.

"Here Jennifer," Tom said, handing his daughter a basket of bread. "Take this to the table."

Tom handed his wife a glass of wine.

"Supper awaits you," he said.

She took a sip from the glass and smiled. They all proceeded to the dining room.

There was almost a glow about them as they talked and dined. Despite all the difficulties of their lives, they functioned in the ideal of the way a good family should carry on. There was no serious tension between husband and wife. There was no problem of discipline with the children. They all loved and respected each other. As rare a thing as this was in the year 2001, Tom Coach knew first and foremost that he was a very lucky man. Years ago, he had married exactly the right woman. They had raised their children well. A family such as this was a rare and frail thing, and Tom treasured it.

Later in the evening, Tom followed Barbara into their bedroom and closed the door behind him. Barbara looked at the bags against the wall, behind the door.

"Are you all packed?" She asked.

"Yes," he replied sitting down on the edge of the bed.

"What time do you have to be at the airport?"

"About ten-thirty would be good."

Barbara took off her skirt and clipped it onto a hanger. She picked up the matching blazer where she had dropped it on the bed and hung it over the skirt, before hanging it in the closet.

"I wish you weren't leaving until Monday," she said. "I'm finally going to have a little time to relax this weekend. I wish you were going to be here."

"That's just the kind of breaks we get . . . Maybe, at least, you'll get some rest. Promise me you'll get some rest."

"Oh, I will."

She stepped into the bathroom.

"You'll never guess what I saw on the train coming home."

"I doubt anything would surprise me," Tom replied.

"There was this young black woman," Barbara continued, "sitting on the floor at the end of the car giving her boyfriend a blow job."

Tom was not surprised. He didn't even bother to mention what he had seen on his way home.

"Believe me," Barbara said, "she was not pretty. He was not pretty. It was not pretty. And do you want to know what I thought? I thought, in a way I don't mind. It gives the creeps and muggers something to focus on besides me . . . I guess I'm getting pretty jaded. You're right; it's getting worse out there. Even in the free love days of the late sixties, when I was Jennifer's age, you didn't see that – not the way we do now. What is it going to be like when our kids are our age?"

Tom didn't answer her. He thought back to when he was a young man, to when he had first come to New York. The city was like cocaine. It made him high. He was addicted to it. Remembering how he had felt then, he saw what the city was to a great many of the people who lived there. To many, it was the highest ideal of what human civilization had to offer. It simply didn't get any better than this. To the people who had been born and raised there, it was home, it was what they knew. What was beyond the city engendered more fear in them than anything they saw on the streets. But he was not one of those people. The city had lost its luster for him. For ten years he had been coasting down from that youthful infatuation he had once known. He was too old now for the night life to excite him. And the benefits of the proximity to the museums, theaters and restaurants was too often nullified by what one had to wade through to get to them.

He took off his slippers and set them beside the bed.

"It doesn't matter to me that we're both at the top of our games in our careers," he said. "I could leave this city right now and never look back."

"Just give me ten more years." Barbara replied. "By then, you'll have your thirty years in and I'll have enough invested that we won't have a thing to worry about. Then you can just give me a town big enough to have a movie theater and a good restaurant and I'll follow you anywhere. We can live right down the road from your parents if you want."

"What would a lady executive like you do in rural Vermont?" Tom mused.

Barbara stopped running the water in the bathroom.

"I'm going to have the most magnificent flower garden ever seen. And you're going to show me how to fish."

"Huh." Tom smiled. "What a dream." He stood up, took off his pants and shirt and tossed them in the laundry basket in the corner. Barbara stepped out of the bathroom and he went in to wash his face.

They were rootless people. Nearly his entire extended family resided in a couple counties in northern Vermont. Her mother spent most of her time in Florida, and her only sibling lived full-time in Denver. But for the love of money, they would raise their children to adulthood in this environment and stay in New York another ten years.

Tom reached for a towel and dried his face. He stood in the bathroom in his underwear and watched his wife's reflection in the mirror as she undressed. He thought about the first time he had ever seen her. He was a college student, sitting in a desk at the beginning of a literature class. He watched her walk through the door of the classroom and hesitate, looking for a seat. Her eyes met his and her gaze stopped right there. She smiled at him and it was love at first sight. He looked at her now in the mirror as she stood naked, facing him. Twenty-two years later, she was still a sight to behold. He hadn't looked at another woman twice in all that time. Home was where you made it. It was where your heart was, and his heart was with her. The first requisite for wherever he would call home was that she would have to be there.

He turned around. She stepped up to him, stood on her toes, reached up and kissed him.

"Looking forward to this is what has kept me going all week," she said.

"Same here."

He took her in his arms and held her close. Whatever lurked in the world outside their walls did not matter. The most important, most loved, most treasured thing in life was what he held in his arms right then.

Ten o'clock the next morning saw them driving

to the airport. The traffic on the expressway was congested and moving miserably slow.

"You've got your ticket?"

"Yes." Tom pulled it from his pocket. "Saturday, September eight, 2001. I believe that's today. Yes, mom, I even packed my toothbrush and clean underwear."

Barbara gripped the steering wheel in her hands and glanced sideways at him in response to his wiseass quip.

"Tell me again how this works," she said.

"Michael and Harvey are picking Ted and me up at the airport in Deer Lake, Newfoundland. The outfitter is putting us up at some motel tonight and we fly out to the camp tomorrow."

"It's too bad you and Ted couldn't have gotten more time off to have driven up with Harvey and Michael. I bet it's really pretty in Maine and Nova Scotia."

"Yeah," Tom sighed. "All for the want of more time. It's the story of our lives."

They pulled off the expressway onto the exit for the airport. There was little relief from the heavy traffic, since it appeared that the airport was the destination for many others as well.

"You haven't said very much about this trip the last few days," Barbara said after some silence. "Are you all right with it?"

"Oh sure. It's not like I'm having some middle-age crisis or something."

"Well, I just wondered."

Tom reached over and put his left hand on her thigh.

"It's just that I haven't done anything like this for a long time. I've got some reservations about being away from you and the kids."

"That's sweet." She smiled at him. "Don't worry about us. You just go on and do this back to nature, cave man thing. We'll be here when you get back."

She pulled the car over to the curb in front of the departures terminal. Tom glanced at his watch.

"Ted's probably checking his luggage as we speak," he said.

He reached over and kissed Barbara.

"Have a good time," she said.

He smiled at her, got out, dragged his baggage out of the back seat and set it on the concrete. Barbara waved at him, put the car in gear and pulled away.

Tom stood and watched his wife drive away. Even though he was only going to be gone a week, he felt a measure of anguish. Whenever they parted, it was disconcerting. She disappeared into the swirling masses in the city and was gone from him, she alone on her way and he on his. No matter how many times he kissed her good-bye and how many years of the routine had passed, he still worried for her. Despite the anticipation of the fine adventure before him, he felt uneasy as he turned and walked through the doors into the terminal. God, he hated airports. You didn't have to be actually lifting off the ground and winging away to some far distant destination to be leaving, he thought. The minute you stepped through the terminal door, you were in a different world – you were already gone.

CHAPTER TWO

My first brush with Tom Coach and his friends came near noon on Saturday. I was on the ferry *Joseph and Clara Smallwood* making the crossing from Nova Scotia to Newfoundland. Halfway across that hundred miles of ocean, the sea was very rough. The passengers mostly milled around in the bar or diner, or like me, slumped in a chair in the lounge listlessly reading the closed-captioned dialogue on the movie screen. Something prodded me from my malaise, saying *"What are you doing vegetating away like this?"* I was far from home, supposedly on a grand adventure. There had to be something interesting to do or see on this boat, if I just got up and went looking for it.

I got up, walked over, hunkered down slightly and looked out the window. *I guess this is what they mean by "gale force winds,"* I thought. I looked down the corridor. The people walking along stepped slowly and tentatively, swaying back and forth, as though staggering from drunkenness, as the ship was buffeted and ever shifted under their feet. I had never been on a ship that size before, so I decided to go outside and see what a storm looked like on the open sea. I staggered over to the stairwell and climbed up the steel steps to the upper level. Pulling my hat down snug on my head, I pushed hard on the water-tight door to be able to open it against the pressure of the wind. It was a real struggle to step outside and shut the door behind me. Outside the whole world was howling. Needless to say, there wasn't another soul in sight anywhere up and down the deck. I leaned against the wall with both hands and slowly made my way out of the lee toward the more open deck. As I rounded the corner of the slippery, wet, steel walk, the hurricane winds caught the bill of my baseball hat and it lifted off into the air and quickly disappeared into the slate gray oblivion, looking like its next stop was the shores of Greenland. I made a hasty grab at it, was promptly flattened by the wind and went sliding across the deck, stopped only by the steel pipe railing from plunging off into the sea. I held on with both hands and pulled my right leg back up onto the deck. *Shiiiiiit, that was close,* I thought. Just then, a wave crashed into the ship, sending a showering spray onto the upper deck where I clung for dear life and the ship lurched toward the starboard side. Something told me it might be a fortuitous time to go with the flow, so I let go of the rail and went rolling and skittering across the deck twenty feet or so, until I banged into the steel plate wall of the crew quarters. As hastily as I could manage, I got onto my hands and knees and crawled towards the door which I had exited a minute and a half earlier. A pair of dusky little birds went frantically hopping before me, against the wall, until they found shelter in the doorway to the crew quarters. I lurched across the open space of the deck to the water-tight door to the stairwell. Reaching up, I got a firm hold on the handle, pulled myself upright, braced hard and muscled the door open. A gust of wind caught the door, and slammed it shut behind me as I scrambled inside.

It was just another fine little example of how one step across a seemingly insignificant threshold could put one in so much peril. I was sprawled with my arms out and my back against the door, when one of the crew members came clanking up the steps. He looked at me in my damp, thoroughly disheveled condition. With my mustache and beard standing out to the sides and me sputtering to catch my breath, I probably looked like Yosemite Sam after he had just made a narrow escape from the lion's pit.

"Are you all right, sir?" He asked.

"Yeah, son, I think I'm gonna survive now," I gasped. "I think it would be a good idea if you issued an advisory about people going outside. I'd sure hate to see any women or children get blown overboard."

The remark was facetious, of course, since I was obviously the only person on the ship foolish enough to have ventured outside.

I straightened myself up, stepped past him, and went back down the stairs to the passenger lounge deck. Stepping across the corridor, I went into the men's restroom. I hunched over, looked in the mirror, and made a few passes at my hair with my hands to straighten myself out. The doors to the stalls were swinging and banging to the rhythm of the storm. I stepped up to a urinal, reeled it out and was leisurely trying to do my thing while dealing with the shifting footing. Another guy came in and parked at the urinal beside me. Just then, another big wave apparently crashed into the ship and the entire vessel lurched.

"Sorry, buddy," the guy next to me said, "but I just pissed on your shoe."

I glanced down and hooted, "Think nothing of it; I just pissed on the other one myself."

We both laughed a little as we zipped up and stepped away. I glanced at the guy. He left the restroom as I was washing my hands. *Average height, fat doofus*, I thought. By the way he was dressed, I guessed he was probably going to Newfoundland moose hunting, like me.

I shuffled back out to the lounge and slumped back into the same seat I had occupied mere minutes before. An announcement in a female voice came over the loud speaker. "The captain strongly advises that due to the weather conditions, all passengers should stay inside for the duration of the voyage." She repeated the advisory in French. *Yeah*, I thought,

I nearly get blown overboard, and then some dickhead pisses on my foot – that's enough excitement for one ferry cruise.

Three hours later, the ship docked at the quaint, little town of Port aux Basques. Looking at the place, I guessed that the number of vehicles driving its streets would be increased dramatically by the cars, trucks and RV's which issued forth from the bow of the big ferry. However, most of the vehicles did just what I did. We drove off the boat, across the staging area and right into a tourist version of the Indy 500 on the one and only highway which led out of town. From the seat of my pickup truck, I took in the stark beauty of Newfoundland at seventy miles per hour. It was obviously a perennially wet place, rocky mountains and rugged, with a dense growth of vegetation. In all my worldly travels, I had never seen another place quite like it. It was a large, unique island which obviously did not have a lot of people residing on it.

That evening, I was settled into a small, semi-dumpy motel in the little town of Pasadena, where I was lodged at the hospitality and expense of the outfitter I had come to hunt with. I had dined alone at a very nice little restaurant, which was probably owned by the fine middle-aged woman I met, who worked there. She was red-haired and bore an uncanny resemblance to me. We had an amiable conversation about our clans. When I left I said, "I'm so very pleased to have met you, Ms. Walsh. You don't know what it means to me to be more than two thousand miles from home and encounter family. We Celts are certainly a far flung race in these times."

"Indeed," she smiled warmly. "Good luck to you."

My experiences of the day had reinforced everything I had ever heard about Newfoundlanders being the friendliest people in the world.

There was a small bar attached to one end of the motel. With it being Saturday night, I thought I would visit with whomever was there and in a social mood, and have a drink before I retired for the night. I went through the little motel lobby, around the cash register and through a swinging half-door into the sparsely furnished bar. There weren't many patrons – a half dozen locals plunking quarters into several video gambling machines against one wall, sipping beer and talking amongst themselves, and four guys like me sitting at a table. I stepped up and leaned over the bar, checking out the options among the liquor bottles.

"Looks like pretty slim pickin's," I said. The four men at the table behind me laughed quietly in response. "Nothing but Canadian whiskey. No offense to Canadians – they're good at a lot of things," I said sideways to the men at the table, "but they can't distill whiskey worth a damn. Now the Irish and the Tennessee hillbillies, they know how to make good whiskey."

"Amen to that," one of the men yelled. I glanced at them and we all continued to chuckle as a short, elderly woman came in through the half-door from the lobby and stepped behind the bar. I had seen her earlier when I had checked in and thus knew that she was a bit of a character. She looked up at me from across the bar. Before she could speak, I asked. "You know, there's something I've been wondering about for the last couple hours or so?"

"Yes?" she said.

"Are you the Little Ole Lady from Pasadena?"

The men at the table burst out laughing. The little, old woman smiled at me in a coy manner, dismissing me as an obvious wise-ass.

"What can I get for you?" she asked.

"Ah – I guess I'll have a beer."

She opened the door of a cooler and asked, "Which kind would you like?"

"Ah, beer's beer. Just close your eyes, reach in and grab one."

She did just that, took my money, then turned to one of the locals at the end of the bar. I took a drink from the bottle and turned around to face the men at the table. That was when I noticed that one of them was wearing a baseball hat exactly like the one I was wearing – one given to me that afternoon by the hunting outfitter.

"I see you fellers are hunting with the same outfit I am," I said, pointing to my hat.

"Angus Wentzell?"

"Yeah. Are you coming out of the boonies, or going in?"

"Hoping to fly in tomorrow," one of them said. He extended his hand. "Tom Coach."

"Tom Coach, " I shook his hand. "Homer Van Meter." I reached around the table from left to right to shake hands as they introduced themselves.

"Ted."

"Harvey."

"Say, I know you," I said. "You're the guy who pissed on my shoe on the ferry."

"Whaaaaat?" Tom asked, as they all laughed.

"What could I do?" Harvey sputtered. "It was rough. The fricken boat lurched and I missed the urinal."

"Jeee-hee-heeez," Ted exclaimed as we all laughed again. Tom looked up at me.

"And you, remember him from that one incident?"

"I never forget a dickhead." I said. "Especially when it pisses on my shoe."

The men fell all over themselves with laughter. All except Harvey, he chuckled and tried to hide it, but he clearly had not taken the remark with the humor I had intended. I noticed the air of insult and it annoyed me. Little did I know then that it was the beginning of a testy relationship between me and ol' Harvey. I shook the hand of the fourth man.

"Michael," he said. "What was it again?"

"Homer."

I studied them briefly. Michael was a small man with glasses, barely more than half the weight of the fat, bald Harvey. Ted appeared to be slightly the tallest and most fit. He was probably five feet eleven, starting to bald, with reading glasses in his shirt pocket. I judged them all to be somewhere in their forties.

"How about you?" Tom asked. "Are you going in or coming out?"

"Like you, hoping to fly in tomorrow, if the weather is fit."

"I understand the state of the weather is everything for bush planes."

"Yeah. Never flown in a bush plane before?"

"No, never," Tom answered.

"You guys?" I asked the others.

"No," were the head shaking responses from Harvey and Michael.

"I have," Ted answered. "Caribou hunting and fishing in Quebec."

"Caribou in Quebec. I did that once – good trip," I said.

"Have you hunted here before?" Tom asked.

"No. I've hunted just about everywhere else on the continent, but this is my first time in Newfoundland. You guys?"

"Never been here before either . . . Maybe we'll end up in the same camp."

"Could be," I said. "I came all alone. This outfitter's got three camps. I'm gonna get thrown in with somebody. Could be you guys."

Everyone seemed comfortable with that notion except Harvey. He seemed to me to have the same kind of petty arrogance as the vice president of a bank where I did business. It was just an initial impression, of course, but in due time, it would prove accurate. I leaned back on the bar and took a drink from my beer bottle. Tom Coach was seated the closest to me and seemed the most willing to converse with a stranger.

"Where are you from?" He asked.

"I live about five miles from a little hick town named Rhinelander, in northern Wisconsin. Own a little one-horse logging company."

"Wisconsin. You're a long way from home. You drove all the way out here by yourself? How long does a drive like that take?"

"Well," I thought, "I reckon it's been eight days since I left home. I took a rather circuitous route, mind you – had some business down in Maine."

"You have logging business in Maine?" Tom asked.

"No – no, not logging business . . . I was visiting a grave . . . Long story."

Tom nodded, not wanting to pry into my private affairs.

"Where you fellers from?" I asked.

"New York," Harvey responded.

"New York City?"

I probably had an edge to my voice when I asked the question.

"Yes, of course," Harvey answered again.

"Ah. Romans," I said, with resignation.

The men looked at each other, perplexed by my remark. I started to turn my back on them.

"Wha – what do you mean, ROMANS," Michael asked?

I didn't want to start an argument or get involved in a long, drawn-out discussion, but I took a drink and decided to respond anyway.

"You're Romans," I said, turning back to face them. "You're living in Rome."

They stared at me with blank expressions. I continued with what I had started.

"There's no finer, more blatant example of the modern city-state. In New York you've got the headquarters for the United Nations, representing the elite of every disgusting, despotic regime on the face of the earth. You've got the Council on Foreign Relations, which for years has provided the script for everything the figureheads running our farcical government in Washington do. And you've got Wall Street and the World Trade Center, arguably the dominant force of the world economy. Between all these you've got the central seat of power for the entire, thinly veiled New World Order design for global government. Even if you're so unobservant and naïve that you choose to believe there's no such thing as the shadow government or a conspiracy, there's no denying that New York is the single most influential city in the world. Face it; it might as well be called New Rome."

I relaxed from my short rant and took another

swig from my beer bottle. The men exchanged glances with each other. I wasn't sure if they were perplexed or offended by my remarks.

"I think you're out on a limb, at least a little bit," Harvey responded.

"I'm – I'm not so sure –" Tom started to say something, but I interrupted him.

"No, no I'm not," I said. I wasn't sure if I was out of line or not, but I had gotten myself into this, so I was obliged to finish. "I surely don't envy you fellers living there though. You couldn't pay me enough to live there. You see, we've come to a point in history where there's three kinds of people in the world. There's Romans, there's subjects, and there's barbarians. Me, I'm a subject. I don't like Rome, but I appreciate living in an orderly society with modern comforts, so I'm fairly content to push for reform by working through the political system. Even though I know the system is rotten to the core with corruption, I'm patient. I'm all for seeking to build a consensus for change, avoiding violence in the process. But out there, on the fringes of the empire, beyond the U.S., Canada, Europe and a few places like Japan, Israel, and Australia, there's hundreds of millions of barbarians who hate Rome. They're constantly funded and goaded by the communists in Russia and China, and the only course of action they know is violence . . . You know, where I live, I sleep fairly sound, secure in the knowledge that nobody is ever gonna go through all the trouble and expense to detonate a multi-million dollar nuclear device just to kill my wife and me, and a couple hound dogs – and maybe a few of our closest neighbors." I paused and took a drink. "We're fast approaching a time when some real heavy-duty shit is gonna start hittin' the fan. If I lived in a major city, like New York, I don't think I'd be sleeping very well at all."

I shifted my stance and took another drag at the beer bottle. That was it, I thought. They would brand me an extremist for sure, now.

"You make a powerful argument," Tom conceded. "You sound a bit like Ted," he said, glancing at his partner.

"Are you an astute observer, Ted?" I asked.

They all chuckled a bit at my remark and shifted glances at each other.

"A freakin' paranoid is more like it," Harvey said.

"I'd like to say I've got a realistic view of things," Ted responded. "I work for the crime lab –"

"Oh. Are you one of those guys who goes out to the scene and dusts for finger prints and stuff?"

"Yes, sometimes." Ted replied. He then started laying out his own hardcore opinion. "I know plenty of police detectives who have no use whatsoever for the United Nations. You wouldn't believe the amount of crime, and suspected crime, that comes out of there; everything from espionage, to rapes and murders. And when they manage to nab some foreign national – they invariably scream diplomatic immunity. So, all we can do is throw them out of the country, and that usually gets done pretty quietly." He leaned back in his chair. "The U.N. is like a frigging Trojan Horse permanently parked inside the city gates – and every time it's time to plug the meter, so they can remain parked there, it's always the American taxpayer that comes up with the change."

"Say, I like you," I said, smiling at Ted. We all laughed. "You and me are gonna get along just fine."

I reached back and set the empty beer bottle on the bar.

"Well, that's it for me. That Parsons feller said he was gonna be here to collect us real early in the morning."

"Before you go," Tom said, "is there a phone here that works, that you know of?"

"Sure. Out here in the lobby – the way I came in. If you've got a credit card to swipe in it, you're all set. It works – I called my wife on it a while ago. I'll show you."

Tom got up and followed me out of the bar.

"There it is," I said. "Apparently the only phone in the whole motel that actually works. Calling the wife?"

"Yeah."

"Well, good luck. All I got was the answering machine. Does a feller good to hear a woman's voice before he heads off into the boonies for a week."

"Thanks," he said. "Good night."

I opened the door, stepped out into the rain and

shuffled quickly off to my room. Tom punched the numbers into the phone and listened to it dial.

"Hello," came his wife's voice from the other end of the line.

"Barbara."

"I knew it would be you before I picked up the phone."

"That predictable, huh? I know it's a little late, but I figured – hey, it's an hour and a half later here and I'm still up."

"I love you."

The small affirmation moved him tenderly.

"I love you too. It seems like a long time since this morning. I just wanted to hear your voice again, before I fly off into the wilderness."

"Go to bed, caveman, and dream about what I'm going to do for you when you come home with that big, juicy, chunk of moose meat," she said, in an intimate, suggestive manner.

"Oooo, now the pressure is on Alley Oop to kill the moose."

She giggled.

"Well, keep the fire burning in the cave and I'll call you when we get back to civilization."

"Sweet dreams."

"Good night."

He hung up the phone and smiled. That guy, Homer, was right, he thought. It does a fellow a lot of good.

CHAPTER THREE

The next morning I awoke to the sound of voices outside. Something told me it was Mr. Gerald Parsons, from the outfitter, come to collect me and the others for the drive to the airport. I got up and looked out the window. It was totally black outside, not even a hint of the sun rising yet. Just then, there was a banging on the door. I opened it to see Mr. Parsons staring blankly at me standing there in my underwear.

"I guess you weren't just fooling around when you said we'd be getting started early," I said in a gravelly voice.

He just continued staring at me.

"Well, I'll be with you in a few minutes."

Mr. Parsons went off, no doubt muttering something to himself that I really didn't want to hear. I staggered into the bathroom and splashed water on my face.

The Deer Lake Airport was a very nice looking little facility. Our little convoy drove right past it to a much smaller building down the road with its own little runway. I had been through this same routine on other excursions before, so I merely parked my pickup truck and walked out to the staging area next to the hangar with my big duffel bag and my rifle case. There were several men standing around in a couple separate groups. The New Yorkers I had met the previous evening were busy unloading the contents of a Chevy Suburban onto the pavement. Tom, Ted and Michael were taking whatever Harvey handed out the back of the vehicle and stacking it in what was fast becoming a very large pile of luggage and gear. I walked over and set down my comparatively very modest baggage.

"You fellers sure you're taking along enough stuff?"

Tom rolled his eyes at me, as he went by with a pair of suitcases.

"We haven't even gotten to the beer yet," he said with an air of slight dismay.

A man who seemed to know what he was doing came out of the hangar with a clipboard and approached me.

"You are – ?"

"Homer Van Meter."

The man looked at his clipboard.

"You're going with them to Angus Lake. Is that your stuff there?"

"Yeah."

"Put it over there with theirs. The plane will be back in a couple minutes, then you'll be going out."

I turned around and Ted shook my hand. He smiled and said, "It looks like we're going to be roomies after all."

"Homer's going with us?" Tom yelled. "Well all right."

I took my duffel over and set it down near their small mountain of baggage. By then they had come out with a full case of liquor and several cases of beer.

"Are you guys going hunting or drinking?" I asked.

"Hard to tell by the looks of all this, isn't it," Tom said. They stacked the last of the beer on the pile and Harvey went to park the vehicle, which was apparently his. I stood with the other three men, surveying the heap of baggage.

"Man," I said, "I wouldn't be surprised if they don't charge you for an extra trip to haul all this stuff out there."

"Do you really think so?" Michael asked.

"I'll tell ya – the last time I flew on a bush plane, was a couple years ago in Alaska. That pilot only allowed two hundred and fifty pounds, including you and your gear. And he had a scale. I was a pound over, and I thought I was going to have to point my revolver at him to be able to take it along."

"We're in trouble," Michael said.

"You think we're in trouble," Ted hooted. "With a two hundred and fifty pound limit, Harvey will have to fly out in his underwear and socks, and leave everything else behind."

Harvey came walking back around the corner of the hangar as the plane came in for a landing. I never ceased to be amazed at what a short landing strip it took for bush pilots to land on.

"A float plane with wheels on it," I exclaimed. "In all my days, I've never seen anything like it."

"It can take off on a runway and land on a lake," Tom commented, no less amazed.

"And vice versa even," Harvey chimed in.

The plane taxied right up to us and killed the engine. The pilot, two men and a woman got out. We helped them unload their baggage and inquired about their success and so forth. Finally, they were all unloaded and leaving, and the pilot turned his attention to us. He stood on the plane's left pontoon, well elevated above us and looked us over. He looked at fat Harvey. He looked at the pile of gear and booze. Since I was taller than the other men, he even gave me a once over. He was not a happy man.

"Are you guys going hunting or drinking?" He asked.

After a fair amount of grousing by the pilot, Tom, Ted and I, with a good share of the baggage, were lifting off the runway, winging northward. I always liked flying in bush planes. At the low altitudes where they flew, you could see a great many interesting things. I thought about the endless herds of thousands of caribou I had seen the last time I had flown, in Alaska. I even remembered the huge, dark, chocolate colored grizzly we had spotted standing on a gravel bar in a river bed, and how he had stood up and pawed the air as we passed a mere hundred feet over his head. Newfoundland was not quite that wild, I thought. I could see a few scattered farms which gradually gave way to forests, cut occasionally by winding ribbons of dirt logging roads. With the lakes and streams and forests, it didn't look so very different than the country where I lived, I thought. There were fewer signs of human habitation, to be sure, but still, I thought, if I had been born here instead, some of those piles of pulpwood and logs down there might be mine.

It was an entirely different experience for Tom Coach. As much as he hated airports and commercial airliners, flying in this little airplane was enthralling. He looked down at the sheer, magnificent beauty of the country and focused on every detail: the yellow-leafed birch trees dotting the coniferous forests, the soggy expanses of muskeg bog, the rocky crags almost alive with the tumbling white water of their rushing streams, and the endless myriad of waterfalls cascading down the mountainsides. He had lived twenty years in the city, surrounded by people and concrete with his nose to the grindstone striving to get ahead. His family and friends recreated when they could at summer vacations spent visiting relatives or Disney World with the kids. The pressure had slowly built in him, over the years, to seek adventure in country like this, and now he was here. This was wilderness. City people like him suffered from a deep, primeval neglect of the animal spirit which clung to hope somewhere in the unknown past of their DNA. The country which passed beneath the wings of the small aircraft was almost an exhilarating nirvana. This was what men like Tom consoled themselves with, by imagining that it was out there somewhere.

The flight only lasted about twenty minutes. The plane settled down into a valley where a fast-running river spilled into a long, narrow lake and then out again at a big rapids. No sooner had I ascertained that this was where were going to land, than we were approaching the surface of the placid water. The pontoons settled into the water as naturally as the webbed feet of a Canada goose and we motored toward a small cluster of modest buildings on the shore. When we were close enough, the pilot cut the engine and we glided toward a rough dock which extended about twenty-five feet out from the shore. Two men on the dock caught the pontoon and secured it with a pair of ropes. The switch of passengers and baggage was a quick, efficient affair; we bailed out and hauled our baggage to the end of the dock, plopped it down, and watched as the guides loaded the gear of those who were leaving.

The guests of the previous week were two elderly couples. Judging by the way they said their good-byes to the guides and the cook, they had had a very enjoyable experience. The four of them got into the plane and they were off. The three guides stood on the dock and waved as the plane motored away, leaving a considerable wake in the otherwise smooth water. When the pilot turned into the breeze and revved the engine to take off, the guides came off the dock towards us. The first one in line extended his hand to me.

"Hello fellers," he said with great gusto. "I'm Cyril, this is Hubert, and that handsome, fine figure of a lad, is Winston."

The old cook came walking down from the kitchen and Cyril introduced him.

"And this fine gentleman is King Solomon. You can call him Sol if you prefers, but it behooves yous to treats him with respect cause ya never knows what he might put in the chow if ya don't."

It wasn't hard to tell that they were a good bunch. We made our introductions and shook hands all around. Then the guides helped us with our gear and showed us our quarters.

The camp consisted of two main buildings elevated on piling about three feet above the ground, a small building which housed the shower and the gas generator, a rather old and rugged looking storage shed, a small screened shelter for hanging meat, and a pair of outhouses. The slightly larger of the two main buildings was the kitchen and quarters for the cook and guides. The other building was our accommodations.

Cyril left us in our cabin after a quick tour of the place.

"Wow," I exclaimed, "these are deluxe accommodations."

"Really?" Tom asked. "I was just thinking they were kind of humble. After all, it's a plywood shack with an outhouse."

I looked at him, a little amazed. Then it suddenly occurred to me that he was not well experienced at this.

"Just how many hunting excursions have you been on?" I asked.

"Well, to be honest, this is the first one."

"You've never been hunting before?"

"Oh sure, when I was a kid in Vermont I hunted fairly often. But the last time I went hunting was in college. I've been a teacher and living in the city for twenty years. Anywhere you can hunt is so far away and a teacher can't get time off in the fall with anything less than an act of God. I had to use up a lot of favors to get this week off to come here."

I was taking my rifle out of the case and examining it.

"Yeah, I know how that is. My wife has been a high school English teacher for twenty-five years now. I know just what you mean about that act of God thing. For nine and a half months a year, she's a sixty-hour-a-week slave to the system."

"English teacher. Really?" Tom asked.

"Yeah."

"I'm an English teacher."

"High School?"

"No, university."

I leaned my rifle in the corner of the room.

"Cool," I said. "I never did ask what all you fellers did for a living."

Ted came in carrying a duffel bag. Tom continued.

"You said you owned a logging company, right?"

"Yeah," I replied.

"Well, I teach English at Columbia. Ted works at the crime lab. Michael's a paramedic, and Harvey's an investment banker."

"Investment banker, huh. Real big bucks type, I suppose?"

"Yes, real hard core Wall Streeter."

"Well, that explains a lot," I said. "Jeez, that's quite a varied selection of occupations. It's just my luck – four guys from New York City and not a single one of you is an editor from a major publishing house."

Tom was dragging a heavy duffel into one of the cabin's three rooms, while I was checking out the wood stove.

"Ted and I are taking this one if that's all right," he yelled.

"Fine," I answered. "I've already got my shit in that one on the right."

"Oh."

Tom came out of the room to fetch another bag.

"Don't tell me you're a frustrated writer," he said.

"Frustrated," I exclaimed. "Frustrated doesn't even begin to describe it. I've always said that I've got tremendous respect for a guy with the urge to write something down and the discipline not to do it. He can sure save himself a lifetime of constant, utter disappointment trying to get published and read."

"Can – "Tom interrupted himself, laughing. "Can I quote you with that?"

Ted was laughing in the other room. "I'm writing that down, right now," he yelled.

"You may feel free to quote away," I said. "It should be a real inspiration to your students."

We went outside where Cyril was standing on the porch yelling and joking. Hubert, perhaps sixty years of age, clearly the oldest of the guides, was sitting on a bench against the outside wall of the kitchen smoking a cigarette. Winston was down toward the lake, beside the old storage building, splitting wood. They were a jovial bunch, of Scottish stock. Their old world accents and manner of speech would, at times, make it a little difficult for us to understand them.

"How old is you fellers?" Cyril asked.

"Forty-seven," I replied.

"Forty-five."

"Forty-six." Tom and Ted replied, respectively.

Though he didn't mention it then, we later learned that Cyril was fifty. He was a strong, fit man, about five feet ten inches tall, weighing about two hundred pounds. His once dark hair was mostly gray and cut in a flattop. He was watching Winston splitting wood and making jokes at his expense. Winston was six feet tall, well built, with fiery red hair and a mustache. He had his ax stuck in a piece of wood and was struggling, trying to free it.

"How old are you now, Winston?" Cyril yelled. He smiled sideways at us and winked.

"Thirty-seven," Winston replied.

"When I was a strapping young lad of thirty-seven, I didn't get my ax stuck in a block of wood."

Winston smiled and took the ribbing in stride. Cyril was obviously a unique and entertaining character. He turned slightly toward us as we stood there for want of something better to do.

"One of the old fellers who just left told me a joke the other day. He says there's this feller who goes to the pharmacy and he says to the druggist that he wants to buy some condoms. Well the old druggist he looks at the feller and he asks him what size he wants . . . Well, the feller, he wasn't expectin' no question like that, so he says – well I don't rightly knows. I never bought no condoms before. So, the druggist he says – well, what ya does is, ya goes out back and ya sees a sheet of plywood with three holes in it. Ya sticks your bill into 'em till ya finds the right size, then, ya comes back and lets me know what size ya needs. Well the druggist's daughter, she hears all this goin' on and she real quick runs out back and when the feller gets his pecker out and pokes it's bill through the hole, she backs up against it. So the feller, he's out there a while. When he finally comes back in, the old druggist he says – well, what size will it be? And the feller he says – to hell with them condoms, I wants to buy that sheet of plywood!"

We all laughed. Even if one had heard the joke before, it couldn't compare with the way Cyril told it.

"That's a good one, ay?" Cyril said. "Now Winston, if ya splits that wood fine enough, I got some glue back here – maybe we can make us a sheet of that plywood."

"You never know what might be on the other side of it out here," Ted joked.

"I tell ya though," Cyril retorted, "if you're out here long enough, a feller might get in the mood to take a gamble on it." He winked at us and yelled at Winston again. "Ya know Wins, when I was a fit young feller of thirty-seven, I didn't have to whack a block of wood twice to split it."

About the time our laughter was subsiding, we could hear the approach of the airplane.

"Well," Cyril said, "I'd say here comes your buddies."

We watched them land and taxi up to the dock, then went to help unload the plane. Harvey and Michael got out and the pilot handed out all the baggage. After we had all the liquor and beer stacked on the dock and the plane was motoring away, Cyril surveyed the heap of booze and exclaimed, "Did ya fellers come to hunt or to drink?"

We had a very nice lunch after getting properly settled in. As we were finishing eating, Harvey got up from the table and asked, "OK, which one of you guys is going to be my guide? It's time to get the rifle out and get to it."

"What, they didn't tell you about the blue law when you met with the outfitter back in town?" I said.

"What blue law?" Harvey said.

"We don't hunt on Sunday in Newfoundland," Cyril said.

"You can't be serious," Harvey said, clearly annoyed.

"It's the law," Cyril stated. "We'll be a huntin' early in the morning. If ya want some exercise, in a little bit we're goin' across the lake with the boats to fetch a bit of firewood."

Harvey turned and walked out of the kitchen. Damn poor form, I thought. Tom, Ted, and Michael glanced at each other. The guides were diplomatic enough to brush it off.

A few minutes later, the guides were making ready to leave with the boats. I came out of our cabin, where I'd gone to fetch a pair of gloves. I looked at Tom and glanced at Harvey, then walked down to join the guides. As we were pushing the boats out into the water, Tom and Ted came down.

"If you've got room, we'll go with you," Tom said.

"Sure," Winston replied, "get in."

The boats were well constructed of heavy wood, about sixteen or seventeen feet long and outfitted with outboard motors. We went across the lake where there was a patch of dead and dying old spruce. While Hubert dropped the dead trees and cut lengths of wood with a chainsaw, the rest of us carried it down to the shore and stacked it in the boats. I was putting a piece of wood in the boat when Tom came down with another piece.

"I suppose those buddies of yours don't figure on burning any wood on this trip?" I said.

"They paid for a hunting trip. As far as they're concerned, firewood is the outfitter's responsibility."

"Typical Romans. Any time there's some honest-to-God, get-your-hands-dirty work to be done – let the slaves do it."

I could see that the remark bothered him, but he was too good a man to defend his friends.

The old cook, Solomon, was indeed a fine gentleman. He was a young looking seventy years old, with a quiet sense of humor. He'd led an adventurous life, working in logging and mining camps, and aboard merchant ships, and he knew how to properly feed a gang of men. We would never see him wear anything on his feet but a pair of slippers. If things got a little too quiet, he had a way of tap dancing around on the plywood floor in the kitchen to liven things up.

When we were finishing with supper, he was tapping and shuffling across the floor when Cyril danced into him. They embraced in the proper pose and glided across the floor.

"By God, Sol old boy, " Cyril said, "with cookin'

like that, if ya didn't snore so loud, I'd have to marry ya."

Having played along, old Solomon just smiled, shook his head and turned to the dishes. Always playing to the audience, Cyril put his hand to his mouth and spoke aside to us.

"For a minute there, I thought he was gonna say – to hell with them condoms, just give me that sheet of plywood."

We laughed and Cyril ducked out the door to attend to something.

Hubert stood up, saying, "Yeeeeah, it's about time." With that short announcement, he stepped over and turned on a small, battery-operated radio. There was no sound distinguishable except for a very loud, annoying static. Cyril came walking back inside.

"That's some radio station you got there, Hubert," I said.

"It'll come on in a minute," Cyril said. "Ya sees, we got so many outposts out here, like this camp here, where's the reception she's not so good. So about this time of the evenin' they cranks up the juice at the radio station and gives us the weather and a bit of the news."

"So you're rather incommunicado here, is what you're saying," Tom said.

"Yayes," Cyril replied. "We got the short wave, but there's no one listenin' at the other end 'cept when the skipper calls us at night to check up on us, and even then 'cause we're in this valley between the mountains, it's tough to be heard. Some nights it's really bad. If you really has to get a message out, we has this cell phone. What ya does is, ya climbs up to the top of the mountain in back of camp. From there, you can get a clear signal and call anywhere in the world."

"Long way to go for a phone call," Ted said. "I gotta get my wife on that plan."

"Here it comes," Cyril said.

Sure enough, the static dissipated and the weather report could be heard fairly clearly. By the attention they gave it, it was obvious the Canadians considered the short, daily report to be important, so we were obliged to be quiet. There was the weather report and a blurb of news. The total duration of the report was no more than three or four minutes, then the radio went to incomprehensible static again.

"She's gonna be good weather tomorrow for moose huntin'," old Solomon said, shutting off the radio.

We sat around the long, narrow table in the kitchen with our glasses and washed the supper down as the sun set over the top of the mountain. The guides and the cook soon drifted away from the conversation into their own society in the back room, near their bunks. They took no care of their accents and colloquialisms among themselves to the extent that their conversation was scarcely interpretable for an American. They sat around a small table where they had a small device for rolling cigarettes and jabbered happily away as they rolled another day's supply of smokes.

Out in the kitchen, we carried on a conversation of our own. It was not typical talk for a hunting camp, I thought. On previous excursions I had made, it did not matter if I was among strangers or friends, the topics were usually the same and the manner was congenial. We seldom talked much about politics, except to cuss politicians. There was no give or take on the matter, because we were all on the same side of the issues of the day. So, in those previous hunting camps we talked about things like guns, ballistics and bullet performance, or our dogs. We swapped endless stories of hunting experiences or discussed plans for the next day's maneuvers.

I quickly assessed that the New Yorkers were not typical hunters and their topics of conversation were not usual hunting camp fare. As a matter of fact, hunting was almost utterly a non-topic for them. I mused, to myself, that the popular question earlier in the day had been conclusively answered. The hunting was incidental to them. No form of the word "hunt" was ever heard between variations of the utterance, "Can I get you another one?" Soon a case and a half of beer, and a bottle of liquor was gone, the conversation turned toward politics, and it was not entirely congenial.

To them, I was a right-wing extremist. To me, Harvey and Michael were commi-liberals. As amazing as it could possibly be to me, they were rabid gun control fanatics, in favor of every registration and confiscation scheme that ever came down the pike. I came to appreciate the presence of Ted right off. He would be termed a moderate by most people. He was a fairly quiet fellow and drank his share of the beer, but by the nature of his training and his career path, he was an objective observer and absolutely non-partisan.

Tom was the moderator. He was also sober. Like me, he had one beer before supper, then switched to juice or water. Politically speaking, he was a member of that forty percent of the electorate who had never paid much attention or formed any solid opinion on most of the issues of the day. He was articulate, intelligent and likeable. I thought his name could just as easily have been John, as in John Q. Citizen; or Joe, as in Joe Average. There was nothing about him that jumped out and grabbed you. He was about 5'10" tall, maybe 180 pounds, brown hair and eyes. You could lose him in a crowd and never catch sight of him again. But if you got to know him a little, it soon became apparent that he was a sincere and caring man who had everyone's best interest at heart. In many ways, he was growing on me.

Harvey had had too much to drink. Nevertheless, he launched into a lengthy monologue extolling the wondrous virtues of the Clinton Administration, and how much the man might have accomplished if the damned right-wing fanatics had just left him alone and not been so concerned about petty things like his sex life. He concluded with saying that he was proud to have voted for the man "both times" and that he was sure that he would eventually be totally vindicated and have history remember him as one of our greatest presidents. Like most political partisans I had encountered, Harvey disappointed me. He raved and ranted like an expert, but his knowledge was superficial and his understanding of what was really going on was shallow at best. I sat quietly, though considerably provoked, and let Harvey rant, knowing that sooner or later he'd get thirsty and have to take a break. I watched Ted and noticed how he quietly squirmed at some of Harvey's remarks. When Harvey eventually wrapped it up and reached for his scotch bottle, I seized the moment with a question to Ted.

"So Ted, in the course of your professional life, did you ever get acquainted with any aspect of the Vince Foster case?"

The question apparently caught him off guard and served to shake him from some mental stupor.

"Interesting question – and I might add an appropriate question in relation to this discussion," he said, glancing at Harvey. "I'm glad you asked me, because I wouldn't have thought of it just now myself."

"Who's Vince Foster?" Michael asked.

"He was the White House Chief Counsel when Clinton first took office," Ted continued. "They found his body in Fort Marcy Park in July of '93 and passed it off as a suicide. But suicide it wasn't."

"I remember about that," Tom said. "Wasn't that one of the things Ken Starr investigated?"

"That's exactly right," Ted said, "good ol' Ken Starr. There never was any real, official investigation – it was a non-stop cover-up from the word go."

"Wait a minute," Harvey said, "you're telling me that the right-winger's boy, their main man, Ken Starr was actually covering up for Clinton when he was investigating him?"

I sat back and watched the exchange, very satisfied with myself. I had asked the right question at the right time and I had an ally to prove my point for me.

"That's exactly what I'm saying," Ted responded. "Starr and everybody else acting in an official capacity with the case covered up the truth in the matter. Myself, I was pretty curious about the case when it happened, but I wasn't involved in any way, so what did I know. Months later, a guy I work with gets his hands on a copy of the forensic report and some scene photos. He comes to work one day and says, 'you gotta see this.' I looked at what he had and it got me going, so I – or we, I should say, reviewed everything else we could get our hands on. The bottom line is the guy was whacked. And the cover up was damned sloppy. I can't believe the case is still being passed off as a suicide. The body was obviously moved to where it was found. The guy is shot twice in the head and neck with a .22, they ditch his body in the park and put an old .38, that can't possibly be traced, in his hand and call it a suicide. The whole thing stinks. I . . ."

Ted was running out of steam, so I jumped in.

"You nailed it, Ted. After previous investigations had ended up questionable at best, Starr hired a guy to do the investigation for him. You know, that's all guys like Starr really do is hire and manipulate a staff that does the actual work. Well good ol' supposedly conservative Ken Starr hired this genuine left-coast, pony-tailed, liberal attorney and after a few months he comes to the same basic conclusion that Ted did. No sooner did the guy reach the conclusion that there was reason to believe that foul play was involved in the whole friggin' case, than Starr dismissed him. The guy was naturally pretty put off, but the mainstream media completely ignored him and he disappeared off the radar screen. Starr subsequently issued his report that the death of Vince Foster was a probable suicide and the case was closed forever."

"Well, what was the motivation for someone to murder Foster and go to all the trouble to cover it up?" Tom asked. "I mean, he was a pretty high-profile guy – someone high up had to want him dead pretty badly to take a chance like that."

"Why indeed, that's the billion dollar question," I said. "It seems most probable to me that it was about the whole fiasco at Waco."

"Bingo," Ted exclaimed.

"Ah come on," Harvey groaned. He was about to start another tirade, but Ted cut him off.

"Let him finish."

"Thanks, Ted," I said. "You see, Foster was really upset about the whole debacle at Waco, really depressed. The official reports even mention that as his supposed motivation for suicide. The thing was, Foster was the official liaison between the White House and the FBI and ATF for the whole affair. He was also a close friend and partner in crime of Bill Clinton since childhood. He knew everything about everything, and one of the things he knew was just what really happened at Waco and it made him sick. After all his years of affiliation with Clinton, he had an attack of conscience. He saw what he was a part of and he couldn't stand it. He was either going to go public, or they thought he was going to, and they whacked him."

"And you're saying," Tom said, "that everything done officially since was a cover up?"

"Yeah."

Ted was nodding in agreement. Michael was squinting, in the middle of some train of thought. Tom was at a loss.

"I just don't see how . . . with all the animosity between the Democrats and Republicans over the Starr investigation and all the money that was spent on it . . . How – how can you say that it was all a sham?" Tom asked.

"What do they care about how much money got spent on the deal. It's our money, not theirs. Look at the details," I said. "Nothing of real substance came from the Starr investigation, just a few minor convictions of characters on the fringes of Clinton's various affairs. And on the point of the case of Vince Foster for instance, who are you going to choose to believe? That's what it is all about – the objectivity. Harvey here, and people like him, preferred to believe that Starr was this crazed conservative whose mission in life was that he was out to get Clinton. People like me sure as hell believed that Clinton needed to be investigated in a major way, but I saw eventually that Starr was part of the problem, not the solution. Back to the point about Vince Foster, here – right here, you've got a friend, Ted, who you know, and presumably trust – a man with the proper experience and training to make a judgment – and he says Foster was whacked. Are you gonna believe him and all the other millions like me, or are you gonna believe a corrupt government scam?"

"You make a powerful case," Tom said, "but what does it all mean?"

"It means we're living in the midst of a deception and manipulation of biblical proportions. The whole reason I brought up this example of Vince Foster was to demonstrate what we're up against. The same people who are committing the crimes are appointing the investigators. That's how powerful and far-reaching the conspiracy is."

"There it is," Harvey blurted out. "I was wondering just how long it was going to take you to get around to playing the old conspiracy card. Tell me this, smart guy, just how can this big, vast, all-powerful, playing both ends against the middle, conspiracy possibly succeed with the kind of news media we've got? There's so much competition for news, that if half of this shit you claim is going on were really happening, they'd be killing each other to do stories on it. Answer me that one, smart guy."

"The major news media is part of the conspiracy."

Harvey slapped his hand on the table and looked at the ceiling. He was a man used to having his own way in a discussion. Both my manner and what I was saying clearly annoyed him.

"If they're in on it, just who the hell is not in on it?" He railed.

"We're not," I replied. "Just think about the news media for a minute. You turn on the TV news at night and what do you see? You'll see something like the O. J. Simpson trial, that the networks will beat to death for months at a time, so they can avoid giving you any real, substantial news. It's not really reporting anyway. Half the time, it's political advocacy and indoctrination. You can switch the channel from CBS to ABC, NBC or CNN and you see the same news stories, told from the same angle – sometimes it's almost word for word the same. The radio is the same way. That's not competition, it's a cartel. It's the same thing with the newspapers. I suspect, you'd be shocked to know the percentage of daily newspapers around the country that are owned by one of just a few major news organizations. Our newspaper, in the little hick town of Rhinelander, Wisconsin, where I live, is owned by the Pulitzer outfit. Last year, I was running for the legislature. I'm a pretty good writer. I wrote a couple articles that got great response. People really liked what I had to say. Then I wrote an article on gun control and how I intended to push for major repeals and reform when I got into office. Boom – just like that the paper stopped running my articles. I wasn't able to publish another thing, and it hurt me bad. The chief editor of the paper was a woman I was pretty well acquainted with – actually a friend of my wife's. We never could get an answer from her about what happened there. My wife actually asked her flat out, at some meeting, what it was all about and the woman just turned pale and turned away. She couldn't answer, because her job was at risk if she did. The answer is obvious. The order came from her superiors to cut me off, and as distasteful as it was for her to do it, if she was interested in keeping her job she had to do it. That's the way it is. They step on bugs like me, before we get a chance to multiply. A few people at the top of a vast organization set the policy for what gets published and who benefits by it."

"But you would think," Michael said, "that with a really big story, some television news magazine would still jump on it. I mean, there's so many of them that there has to be some independence there."

"Very little independence, I'm afraid." I said. "TV is the most controlled news environment that there is. Look at the big name personalities who do the reporting and think about it. The phenomenon of the TV news superstar is a fairly recent development. These people didn't get to where they are completely on their own. They got there because they held certain views or because they were willing to toe the line. And below them are all kinds of up and comers who would do anything to have that kind of money and prestige. If they have to toe a certain line to make the cut, they do it."

Everyone was very involved in the discussion. At the very least, I had provoked serious thought. Harvey started to say something, but I cut him off.

"Remember Walter Cronkite – good ole America's most trusted newsman, Walter Cronkite. Remember how at the end of the broadcast, every single evening, he would utter the same line – 'And that's the way it is, Friday, November twenty-second, nineteen sixty three' – or whatever date it was?"

"Yeah, I remember that," Michael chimed in. "He said it exactly the same way, every single night, at the end of the news."

"That's right," I continued. "Well, good ol' Walter published his memoirs a couple years back, just to come clean, I guess, before he kicked off. The most noteworthy thing he had to say was, that when he uttered that now famous line at the end of every broadcast, he frequently knew that that wasn't the 'way it is'. He owned up to the fact that he willingly lied to the American people, on a regular basis, to promote an agenda which he usually agreed with. So there you have it – straight from the horse's ass mouth, of America's most trusted news anchorman, that the news was frequently nothing but propaganda. And it hasn't gotten better. What we have now is a news apparatus that would make Joseph Goebbles proud."

There was a lot of resigned sighing and nodding of heads.

"Well, I just don't think your whole conspiracy theory holds water," Harvey said. He reached for his bottle and poured himself another drink. I couldn't help noticing that he took his drinking so seriously that he had even brought his own set of cocktail glasses.

"Oh, it's not a theory. Theory means that you're dealing with some unproven hypothesis. I'm quite certain of my knowledge. I might have some unsubstantiated suspicions from time to time, but I winnow it down to objective truth before I spout off about it, like this."

"Well you've got your man Bush in office now, so I guess it's all behind us anyway."

I looked at Harvey incredulously.

"You haven't heard a damn thing I've said."

They all looked at me and it became obvious that I had indeed failed to make my point.

"Are you telling me that George W. Bush is not your man? That you didn't vote for him?" Harvey asked, as though incredulous.

"That's right."

"Well then, what the hell is all this blather about?" Harvey yelled. "Who the hell did you vote for?"

"If you really want to know, the wife and I voted for Harry Browne, the Libertarian candidate. We're not members of the party and don't believe in absolutely everything they stand for, but in this particular election, it was the only palatable choice."

"That's not a legitimate vote," Harvey thundered. "That's anarchism."

"Sadly, that's the current state of affairs of American politics. Between the Democrats and Republicans they own the playing field and they're both puppets of the same masters." I said, "about the most positive thing I can say about Bush is that he's not Clinton. I sure enough hated Clinton – still do. I believe in defining moments in history. For me, the defining moment for the American society, for the New Roman society if you will, came on Friday, February twelve, 1999 . . . That was the day when the Senate voted in the impeachment trial of Bill Clinton and decided to let him off. That was the day the handle was tripped and we all started spiraling down for the big flush down the toilet – the point of no return."

"Ah, jeez," Harvey groused.

I didn't let him stop me.

"Clinton was a lying, raping, murdering, treasonous piece of shit. When a congress of our supposed representatives can't work up the gumption to pass the hat to take up a collection, to buy a pair of balls, to boot a piece of human slime like that out of office – well, we've gone back to the days of Caligua and Nero."

As sad a statement as it was, it nevertheless elicited laughter. Even Harvey smiled as he took another drink.

"However," I continued. "The first time most of us heard the words *New World Order* was when they fell out of George Bush Senior's mouth. I didn't trust him and I don't trust his son. It's obvious that both of the Bushes and Clinton were and are all slaves to the same masters and they pursued and continue to pursue the same agenda, albeit in a slightly different manner."

"Don't get me wrong," Harvey said. "I'm not agreeing with you on everything else, but you gotta be right about the part of George W. being a puppet. Every time I see the guy on TV, it's obvious that the man is a blithering idiot. He's a moron, he couldn't bend over and tie his shoe by himself. Somebody's gotta be telling him what to do."

"Well, Harvey," I said, "maybe in some small way, I've made progress with you."

That brought chuckles from everyone. Tom, the

moderator, had been sitting quietly, digesting all that was said.

"If there's a conspiracy, who are they? What do they hope to accomplish?" he asked.

"They're little munchkins, running around in Homer's mind," Harvey joked, "and their goal is to steal our beer. I think I'll go out and piss on them right now." He got up and went outside. Michael poured the last of the scotch from the bottle into his glass and Ted cracked open another beer. Tom wasn't happy with the level of his friends' alcohol consumption. He reached for a pitcher on the table.

"More water, Homer?" As he filled my glass, then his, he repeated his question. "So, who are they, what are their goals?"

"Like any big organization, there's a pyramid of power. At the very top, I suspect there may be no more than a dozen men globally. It's nearly impossible to say definitely just who they are, and I have no doubt they work hard to keep it that way. If you slide down a notch, though, it becomes more obvious."

Harvey came back in and sat down. I had everyone's attention, so I continued.

"In the United States, we are principally talking about the Council on Foreign Relations."

"Oh that was the group you mentioned last night," Tom said, "that you said was headquartered in New York."

"That's right, in a building called the Pratt House that they built back in the 1920's."

"They've been around that long?"

"Yeah, gives you an idea how well established they are and how long they've had to build a power base. Anyway, they're a group of the wealthy elite who are the real power in our country. They like to pass themselves off as merely being a think tank, but that doesn't quite get it. Their membership is . . . I think somewhere in the neighborhood of 3600 people, and if you look at the list, it reads like a veritable who's who of the leaders of the federal government, business, banking and finance, academia, and the major news media. All of the congressional leaders in recent years have been members, as well as nearly all of the cabinet members. It's well known in some circles, that a prerequisite to being promoted to the rank of general in our military is membership in the CFR. In most presidential elections, both the Democrat and the Republican candidates will be members. They put on a good show of being opponents, but it really doesn't matter which one gets elected, because the same agenda is pursued, just in a slightly different fashion to put on a good show of bending to the will of the electorate."

"You're saying the only thing elections are to them is a barometer of how much they can get away with?"

Tom's interest grew in intensity as he asked the question.

"Exactly. They have a number of committees and

commissions, and if you take a very close look at what comes out of these little meetings of the elite, behind closed doors, you see the establishment of policy and legislation which invariably controls the direction our government takes. Our government is a sham, a showpiece, something to be manipulated by the CFR. The CFR is the shadow government. They're power mongers to say the least, and when you've got one of their minions like ole Strobe Talbot, Clinton's number two man at the State Department, going around giving speeches saying that in fifty years time the United States will cease to exist as a sovereign nation – that it will merely be just another state in a one-world, global government – well, I'd say that their intentions are pretty thinly veiled. Everything they do leads incrementally in that direction. If you are naïve enough to believe that a one-world government is desirable, I think you need to seriously ask yourself just whose one-world government is it going to be? If you ask me, it's like Lord of the Rings in very real life. I would never willingly grant anyone or any small group of anyones absolute power. Absolute power is usually followed by absolute corruption. There isn't a doubt in my mind that when we have a one-world, global government, we will have global tyranny."

"I think you're out on a limb," Harvey said. "I know a couple of those Council on Foreign Relations guys."

Everyone looked at him.

"How do you know them?" Tom asked.

"I work for 'em. They own my bank. There's nothing nefarious about them. Hell, every once in a while they give me great stock tips."

"Uh huh, I'll bet you've never lost on one of their tips either, have you?" I said.

"No, never. You can't beat 'em."

Everyone was looking at Harvey in amazement.

"What?" he yelled.

"Well, gentlemen, I oughta rest my case right here," I said. "Ole Harvey is on the verge of proving it for me. He's a fine example of how these people's manipulations reap certain profit and as long as they dole out some small favors to the Harveys of the world every now and then, the Harveys will be happy to turn a blind eye to their excesses."

"I don't know," Michael said. "I just can't buy it. There's probably some truth to some of your claims, but overall, it's just too far out there. I just can't buy the overall claim of a conspiracy of that magnitude running the country."

"I can," Ted said. "I knew it already. I've just never heard it laid out this concisely before. You've got your shit together on this, man," he said. "Before we leave here I want to know some of your sources of information."

"Thanks, Ted. I'll see what I can put together."

"I'm not sure what I think," Tom said. "I don't want to believe you're right. I mean, it paints a pretty undesirable portrait, but still, some of what you're saying can't be ignored . . . I guess I just need more proof."

"I don't quite know what to do to make true believers out of you. If I take your addresses and go home and send you off reading lists and reams of articles and literature, you won't want to spend the time to comb through it all. And if you do, you'll probably just dismiss it as so much propaganda." I thought for a moment. "What if . . .Would you accept that proof of a conspiracy would be that you could predict what they were going to do based on long, careful observation of their past activities?"

"I guess that would depend on the prediction," Tom said.

"Well, there is one thing of significance which I've become certain of fairly recently. I've already bothered my wife and some of my friends back home with it, so I'll lay it on you guys, and days, weeks or months from now when it happens, you'll keep in mind that I told you it was going to happen."

"Well," Harvey said, "that's a real specific time frame. Are you sure you wouldn't like to go for sometime in the next half century just to cover your ass?"

"All right, you want specifics, I'll say within two days to two years, probably within the next six months. I can't get any more specific than that."

Harvey was hesitant.

"Hell, you don't even know what he's talking about yet." Ted said. "Let him finish."

"All right, here goes," I said. "Back in 1998, with the blessing of Bill Clinton, the Council on Foreign Relations set up a commission headed by former senators Gary Hart and Warren Rudman. This commission came up with this grandiose plan for a new cabinet level department called the National Homeland Security Agency. The whole monstrous plan, if you ask me, looks like 1933 all over again, when the Nazis came up with "Fatherland Security" legislation. They burned down the Reichstag Building and blamed it on a drunk communist to whip up enough public support to pass it. Once this Nazi plan became German law, history came to know it as the "Enabling Act." It enabled Hitler to do all kinds of draconian stuff that couldn't be gotten away with before."

"You're losing me here," Tom said. "What's that got to do with us?"

"Well, shortly after Bush took office, some members of this Hart-Rudman Commission delivered copies of their proposal to the White House, and presumably had a pretty good parley with the new pres about it. And remember what I said before – these people don't merely make idle suggestions – they dictate, and their middle-management puppets toe the line."

"You're saying that Bush is just middle management."

"That's right."

"OK, go on."

"I've got this buddy named Ed. Ed's famous for getting the inside scoop on things like this long before it becomes general public knowledge. Well, Ed got a copy of this Homeland Security proposal and read the whole long, detailed, boring blueprint. He came to see me a couple months ago and we went fishing – sat out in the middle of the lake and had a long discussion about the implications of all this. We decided that sometime in Bush's first four years in office, probably sooner than later, these bastards are gonna engineer some kind of a terrorist attack to whip up public sentiment so they can implement this plan."

Tom was on the edge of his chair, thinking.

"So, you're saying they're going to . . . blow up a major building or maybe dump biological or chemical toxins on a city, or – "

"A suitcase nuke, maybe. Who knows. All I can say is, when it happens, it's going to be big – big enough to galvanize the whole country."

"And it will be our own government who does this to us?" Tom asked.

"Well, not the government exactly – the conspiracy – the power behind the government."

"And they're going to carry it out themselves, and blame it on some patsy, or patsy organization?"

"Either that, or we also know that they have deliberately shut down FBI and CIA investigations of communist funded, Islamic fundamentalist plots and so forth. It well could be that they'll just let something, or encourage something to happen that's already out there. That would also fit in quite well with their plans to drum up an excuse to start a war in the Middle-East."

"Why would they want a war in the Middle-East?" Michael asked.

"Because there's a huge chunk of the world over there that has utterly refused to get on board their plan for a one-world government," I said. "It's going to take some coercion and changes in their governments to assimilate them into the scheme."

They were quiet with their thoughts for a moment.

"There is one thing my buddy, Ed, talked about which has lately got me to thinking," I said.

"Yeah?" Tom asked.

"Yeah," I continued. "I thought it was maybe a little – out there – when he first talked about it, but, after some thought . . . I think it's just possible that Ed is onto something."

They all looked at me expectantly.

"You see, Ed is an airline pilot. He's the kind of pilot you'd want to have flying the plane you were on. He doesn't just stumble out of the airport bar, plop down in the cockpit and take off. Before every flight, he gets down on the tarmac, walks around the plane and checks things out – sometimes even kicks the tires."

"What's that got to do with anything?" Harvey snorted.

"Well. He was telling me, back in late May, or early

June – somewhere about that time, he was in Boston . . .

"At Logan Airport," Michael volunteered?

"Yeah," I continued. "He was at the airport in Boston, walking around the plane, doing his thing, looking everything over while they were loading the luggage on, and he chanced to look over at the plane parked next to his . . . and he saw this thing protruding from the fuselage under the cockpit. It stopped him in his tracks. Now, keep in mind this is a guy who eats, drinks, and breathes airplanes. He knows everything about every model of plane ever manufactured. And what he was looking at just didn't belong there. He described it as looking like a ball turret attached to the underside of the cockpit."

"How big was it?" Tom asked.

I started to answer, but Harvey butted in again.

"Again. What the hell has this got to do with anything?"

"I'm gettin' to that," I replied. Looking at Tom, I said, "I think he said it was a little bigger than a basketball. Anyway, he walked over and stood there for a while looking at this out of the place apparatus on the airliner. He said it looked like it had a camera in it and he figured maybe it was mounted so that it could rotate and get a view of things. He had never seen or heard of anything like that before, and suffice it to say that he was really intrigued. So he started asking around about it. It wasn't easy but he finally found a guy who knew something about it. The guy told Ed it was part of a system they were experimenting with to fly the plane by remote control. The guy said some rudimentary technology like this had been around since the late 70's, but they – the military specifically – were really ramping up the research and development of this technology. He told Ed that within just a few years, he figured the military would be flying these pilotless aircraft around and bombing the enemy with them – completely by remote control through a satellite connection – with the plane being one place, and the pilot sitting at a control console, maybe thousands of miles away."

"Oh, no way!" Michael exclaimed. He and Harvey were shaking their heads in disbelief. Tom started to ask something. I held up my hand to urge patience.

"I'm getting to it," I said. "Yeah, that's what the guy told Ed. Ed said the guy was exceptionally knowledgeable and seemed certain of what he was telling him . . . so Ed, naturally, asked the guy what the contraption was doing on a commercial airliner. They guy replied, without hesitation, that there were some high muckey mucks who thought it could be useful if a plane was hijacked. They could just take over the flying of the aircraft from afar – in effect seize control of the plane no matter who was in the cockpit."

"Jeez," Tom said, "that's just . . . scary,"

"No shit." I said. "Needless to say, Ed saw the nefarious potential for the setup right off . . . Which brings me to the other thing Ed told me . . . Several years ago, when he was between pilot jobs, Ed spent a couple years as a flight instructor . . . So he knows these other flight instructors, and he flies around all over the country and talks to all these other pilots; and he started hearing about this bunch of Arabs that are in these flight schools around the country. There's more than one guy he talked to that figures there's something just not right about these guys."

"What do you mean?" Tom asked.

"Well, you know, learning to fly is usually one of those things that people do only if they are really gung ho about it. This bunch of Arabs – there must be about fifteen or twenty of these guys as near as Ed is able to glean – are apparently, by all observations, just not really all that interested in actually learning to fly a plane. One instructor who had several of these guys for students told Ed it was just like they all didn't really give a shit. Said he never saw anything like it. Said they all kinda just kept to themselves, were semi-antisocial and really were just going through the motions – like somebody was paying them to be there, and they were just puttin' in their time."

"What the –" I put up my hand and cut Harvey off.

"Just indulge me a little bit longer. I'm getting to it."

Harvey wasn't the only one getting restless. I knew I had to wrap it up.

"So anyway, Ed thought all this was sufficiently

suspicious that he did a lot of asking around, and he discovered a couple really disconcerting things about these guys. On at least one occasion, several of them were flown across the country in a jet that was chartered by the CIA."

"No shit?" Ted asked.

"Yeah," I continued. "And it gets even better. A while back four or five of 'em got into a fight in a bar – somewhere in Florida, I think it was. The local cops threw 'em in jail. And – bing, bang, boom, just like that, within a couple hours, a bigshot from the FBI showed up and told the cops to turn 'em loose."

"Really," Ted exclaimed.

"Yeah. Taken altogether it's just a damn suspicious proposition . . . So, to finally cut to the chase: back in July, when Ed and I were sitting down on my dock fishing, and comparing notes on this upcoming terrorist event which we are nearly certain is coming, potentially any day now, he laid out how he figured it was most likely gonna go down. He figures a commercial airliner, or maybe even a couple of them, are gonna get hijacked by remote control and maybe crashed into something, like a stadium full of people, or maybe a tall building somewhere – like the Sears Tower in Chicago, or the Empire State Building in New York – you know, the list of potential targets is almost endless."

"And then they'll blame it on these shiftless Arabs for patsies." Ted said.

"Exactly," I replied. "And there you have it, the

perfect setup for swaying public opinion so they can pass any number of draconian laws, and have a pretext for going to war in the Middle East."

"And who exactly do you think will pull this off?" Tom asked.

"The CIA. Probably with the help of the Mossad?"

"What's the Mossad?" Michael asked.

"The Israeli version of the CIA." Ted replied. "Except they're nastier."

"And you think our own government has elements in it which would actually, callously murder its own citizens just to promote a political agenda." Tom said with resignation.

"Not a doubt in my mind," I said.

"God," Tom concluded. "I'm going to remember that you told us this. I sure hope you're wrong, but I'll remember."

"I hope I'm wrong too, but I'm not." I said. "I sure feel sorry for whoever the victims of this are going to be."

"So let me get this straight," Harvey said. "What you're saying is, that on the basis of some lunatic prediction by a couple super-paranoid, red-neck doofusses named Homer and Ed, we're all supposed to be quaking in our shoes over the completely whacked out threat of what our own government – or excuse me – the evil conspiracy behind our government, is going to do to us?"

"That's pretty much it. To quote an old guy named William S. Burroughs, 'A paranoid is a man who knows a little of what's going on.' Believe me, Homer and Ed make it their business to know what's going on."

"Well I've got another quote for you," Harvey said, standing up. "Paranoia will destroy ya. That's enough for me. I can't believe I actually sat here all this time and listened to this bullshit."

"Look at it this way," Tom said, as Harvey was going out the door, "it gave you something to do while you were pouring a bottle of scotch down your throat."

He turned and looked at me as Michael and Ted got up and left.

"I'm sorry about him. He drinks too much."

"You don't have to apologize. I've played this scene before."

We got up and were walking out when Cyril stuck his head out of the back room and called after us.

"When ya hears the generator fire up in the morning, you can get up and come over, and we'll have a good breakfast before we heads out."

"OK. Thanks," Tom yelled back.

Outside it was dark and cool. The prevailing sound was that of the gasoline powered generator. Tom and I stood several feet apart, facing the lake, urinating before we went to the cabin to retire for the evening.

"I'm going to think about what you said," Tom said. "I'm not going to pass judgment on it without some time to think about it. I just want you to know that."

"Fair enough," I replied.

We went into the cabin and headed straight for our bunks. As I settled into my sleeping bag, I was disappointed with myself. I had not stood up well to provocation, I thought. I had wasted my time and gained little, except for the respect of Ted, who was already on my side to begin with. Maybe Tom was worth the trouble, but there was no way I was ever going to persuade guys like Michael and Harvey to my way of thinking. They were Romans, they were foreigners to me.

In the back of my mind, I went back in time to a little over a year before. I had been giving a speech in the course of my campaign for the legislature. When I came down from the podium and sat down next to my wife, she leaned over and said, "Real smooth on the delivery there, Slick." It was her way of saying that I had gone off on the wrong tangent. It wasn't as if I hadn't done it before. Back in college, my friends and acquaintances had voted me the most likely to exceed. Though I realized that it was not a complimentary title, all these years later I was still doing it. Perception is a difficult thing to alter, and it is all important to persuasion. It didn't matter what I thought, obnoxious is in the eyes of the beholder.

Even though I had been lying down only a few minutes, I was very uncomfortable. I was too tall for the bunk. My feet were hanging over the end and a board down there felt like it was about to cut them in half. Disgusted, I got up and turned on the light. Just then, the generator died and the light went out.

"Damn it to hell," I yelled.

"Are you all right over there, Homer?" Tom called.

"Yeah, just making some adjustments. Like everything else in the world, these bunks are made for runts."

I found my flashlight, turned it on, slid my sleeping bag off onto the floor, grabbed the mattress off the empty bunk next to me and threw it onto my bed. I rearranged my sleeping bag and crawled back into it. There, that was much better, I thought. My feet were still hanging over, but at least they were elevated enough that the troublesome board was no longer a bother.

As I settled down for the second time, I thought of my wife again. There was a natural, unwritten law which said that one of the prime functions of a spouse was to moderate behavior in its mate. In the back of my mind, I could hear that loving, nagging voice saying, "Real smooth on the delivery there, Slick."

CHAPTER FOUR

When the sound of the generator being started up jolted me awake the next morning, I looked up and out the small window into a pitch black sky. I was typically a pretty slow starter in the morning. Nevertheless, I got dressed and stumbled to the kitchen for breakfast with considerable ease compared to the hung-over New Yorkers. We were sitting at the table eating our fried eggs and bacon, when Harvey finally tottered in, all bleary-eyed and flopped down.

Tom looked at him with a big smile and goaded him.

"Isn't it a beautiful morning, Harvey?"

"Oh fuck you."

"I second that," Michael replied.

Tom glanced at me and we smiled broadly at each other.

In due course, with the outhouses having done a big business, everyone was properly coffee'd up and ready to go. Being somewhat of a victim to a lifelong concession with being ruled by my bowels, I was the last one to be ready. By then, the sun was well up and Tom and Cyril were the only ones left in camp, besides the old cook, of course.

I grabbed my rifle and a small knapsack and joined Tom in front of the kitchen. The guides, being old pros at sizing up the interests and physical capabilities of their clientele, had made their decisions the night before.

"Everyone's left, huh?" I said.

"Yes," Tom replied. "Ted and Michael went with Winston in a boat up the lake. Hubert took Harvey in tow and went off in that direction, down the lake. Cyril is taking us up the mountain."

"Good, I was hoping to go that way."

"It's been a lot of years since I've climbed a mountain," Tom said with some reservation. "I hope I can keep up with you outdoors types."

"Did you do any physical conditioning . . . Outside of jumping the wife's bones, I mean."

"Yeah, plenty of that," he smiled. "I ran around the block a couple times a day for the last six weeks – which isn't as easy as it sounds in New York."

"Ah, you'll do fine then. It'll be like your boyhood days in Vermont, except wetter. What's your preference for a moose?"

"Well, I'd like to shoot one."

He didn't know what I meant by the question.

"I mean are you looking for a big one, a little one, or any one? It would be good for us to have our preferences sorted out before we get up the hill.

Sometimes things happen pretty fast when you spot the game, you know."

"Oh, I see what you mean. Well, I'd like to shoot a nice bull, with good-sized, palmated antlers. I guess I'd hold out for one like that, at least for the first two or three days."

"We're compatible then," I said. "I'd prefer to shoot a younger bull. You can't eat antlers and a younger one makes for more tender chow. As a matter of fact, my wife gave me instructions, in no uncertain terms, to not come home with a hundred year old critter that was going to be like chewing on a radial tire."

"I thought we would be flipping a coin or something for the first shot at a big bull."

"Not necessary," I said. "It's yours."

"Are you absolutely sure about that? That's being awfully generous."

Tom was holding his rifle up, looking through the scope.

"Not nearly as generous as you might imagine. I'm after proper chow."

"Is moose that good?"

"It has a definite edge on beef or anything else, and the only way you can get moose meat is to whack it yourself. That's what it's all about," I said. "If you want to eat really well, you've got to go out and hunt the chow down yourself."

Tom laughed.

"It sounds like you're a real aficionado of wild game meat," he said.

I was stuffing cartridges into the magazine of my rifle.

"You got it. I've got this hunting buddy from Pennsylvania. He's got it figured that just about the biggest insult to a guy's manhood is to be so unsuccessful at hunting that you're reduced to eating beef."

Tom laughed.

"So, have you and your missus been living in wedded, gastronomical, beefless bliss?"

"Twenty-four years now and haven't had to buy beef yet. Hopefully it will remain that way 'till death do us part."

"How about your buddy?"

"I'm afraid he got divorced a while back. I think he was spending too much time hunting."

Just then, Cyril came out of the kitchen.

"Are ya fellers ready to head out?"

"We are for a fact," I said.

"Very well," Cyril said, shouldering his pack, and picking up a small ax. He turned to call into the kitchen. "If we gets a moose early, we be back for lunch. If not, we sees ya this evening."

Solomon came to the door and said, "Good luck now to you fellers."

We fell in line behind Cyril and started off. After a few steps, he stopped and turned around.

"Just one thing," he said. "The proper way to carry

your rifle is with the magazine loaded and the bolt closed on an empty chamber. That way, if ya slips and falls you won't accidentally shoot each other or your old guide, Cyril – and there's plenty of places to slip and fall."

I nodded to Cyril that I was already in compliance. Tom opened his bolt and removed the cartridge from the chamber, then slid the bolt closed on an empty chamber.

"Good," Cyril said. He took two steps then turned around again. "Just one more thing. If yous are up there lookin' around with your bifocals and ya happens ta sees a sheet of that plywood, make sure ya sings out real loud and clear. Ta hell with them condoms, ay."

What a character. We laughed and started off again.

It was fairly easy walking initially. We traversed the gently sloping, wet, moss-covered ground and followed a rough trail hacked through the occasional patches of spruce, stepping over several rivulets of trickling water and around deep, stagnate pools. Cyril stopped beside one small pool and turned to us.

"We calls these things Newfoundland bathtubs. Some of the little ones a feller could actually take a bath in, ay. But there's an awful lot of 'em, like this, where ya wants to watch your step. It seems there's no bottom to 'em. If ya slips in this mud and falls in, ya may never be seen again."

It wasn't hard to tell, by the way he said it, that

it was a serious warning. The bathtubs were most likely chutes formed by escaping magma and hot gasses during volcanic activity in the far distant past. These chimneys, possibly hundreds, or even thousands, of feet deep were then filled with water in later epochs.

A few minutes later, we stopped again at the edge of an open area. It was more sloped and literally strewn with "bathtubs". In all my travels and experiences, I had never seen anything even remotely like the dark, foreboding pools of water. They were apparently a hazard which was unique to Newfoundland. Cyril turned to us again.

"We calls this place Wet Ass Hill. It's got the combination of mud and slope that can make it a rough go. Many a feller has slipped and fell and got a wet ass here – that's why we calls it the way we does. Near lost a hunter in one of the tubs a few year back. Ya watches your step here, ay."

Tom turned and looked at me.

"No matter where you go, there's always something," I said. "If it ain't cliffs, crevasses in the glacier, rattlesnakes or grizzly bears, it's the friggin' Newfoundland bathtubs."

Tom followed Cyril, and I followed him. We were careful of our footing and managed to climb and traverse the expanse while staying upright and dry. It gradually became more steep and rocky in places. Cyril was a fit man who obviously had no aversion to sweating and breathing hard. He set a pace which kept us working to keep up.

The trail was such that in places the bushy, knee-high scrub was sufficiently dense and entangling that it precluded actually seeing where one placed his foot. It was in one of these tangles on a steep portion of the climb, where Cyril suddenly pitched until he nearly fell and yelled, "Damn!" He leaned on his ax with one hand and held up one foot. We stopped behind and slightly below him, as he parted the bushes with his left hand and swung the ax with his right. With the hammer side of the ax, he struck a rock several times.

"There, it won't do that again," he said. "That sharp rock punched a hole clear through the heel of me boot. It just goes to show ya, it don't matter how many times ya walks the trail, every once in a while she'll have a surprise for ya."

"Is your foot all right?" Tom asked.

"Yayes. But the boot is not so good."

Indeed, the knee-high, green-colored, rubber boot had an irreparable gash in it and Cyril was noticeably perturbed because of it.

"Got another pair back at camp?" I asked.

"No. That's all right. I'll just have a wet foot for a while I reckon."

He turned to resume the climb when from somewhere in the expanse of mountainside below us, we heard an audible "whump".

"Was that a shot?" Tom asked.

Cyril turned and gazed out over the country below us.

"Yayes," he said. "I'd say your old pal Harvey just got a moose. That came from the direction Hubert was taking him."

Tom turned and looked out over the rugged terrain. There was nothing moving anywhere in the forest below to give any accurate notion of just exactly where the sound came from or exactly what had transpired.

"Well, it would be great luck if he actually killed a moose, but he might have missed."

"No," I said, "it was a close shot. The bullet traveled no more than twenty or thirty yards, and it struck a big chunk of meat solidly."

"Yayes," Cyril said, matter of factly. "It's a dead moose."

Tom looked perplexed.

"Something wrong?" I asked.

"It's just that you both seem to be so absolutely certain of what happened, just from a faint sound that I can only guess was a shot, because I don't know what else it could be. How is that possible?"

"Experience," I said. "Long-time observation."

We turned and resumed our climb.

Far below us, in a small clearing in the spruce forest, Harvey had indeed shot a moose. The weathered, lean old guide, Hubert, had led the arrogant, profusely sweating, falling over every obstacle city-slicker on the most gentle, easily traversed path he knew into prime moose habitat. They had just hopped across a rather noisy, fast-falling rivulet and come to the edge of a little, sparsely grassed opening, when the old guide saw a faint flicker of movement across the clearing. He immediately held up the ax in his left hand and turned to Harvey with his right index finger to his lips. The two men froze in their tracks for a long minute and a half, before Hubert saw the unmistakable flash of polished antler tips move slightly amidst the spruce branches. He turned again to Harvey and indicated for him to load the chamber of his rifle and cautioned him to be very quiet. Harvey worked the bolt very slowly and loaded the gun. Hubert grabbed him by the shoulder and urged Harvey to step just ahead of him and crouch down. Harvey's heart started pounding and his blood pressure went off the gauge. When he was in position, Hubert leaned and spoke softly in his ear, "Wait 'till 'es in the open and standing still." Then Hubert cupped his hands to his mouth and grunted twice in a manner which years of experience had taught him was sure to get the desired response.

The bull was totally oblivious to the presence of the men. He was in the last year of his life. His eyes were poor, his teeth were ground down to nearly nothing and he was far too lean to survive the coming winter. He was trying to get through his last breeding season without having to engage in serious combat with younger, stronger bulls. When he heard the grunts from across the clearing, he was angered by the sound of another bull, an interloper in his territory, calling cows to him. In his younger days, he would have immediately trotted out, shaking his head and huge antlers, ready to do battle. Now, however, he moved tentatively. He stepped out into the clearing and turned toward the place where the sound came from. Slowly, one step at a time he approached, his head held high, with his big antlers rocking from side to side. It was an awesome and intimidating sight. Any bull not possessing the gonads to do serious battle would have turned tail and run for it. As intimidating as his seven foot high antler tips were, it was not quite enough to run off Harvey. Harvey's entire system was revved so high it was about to throw a rod and his blood pressure was beyond the red line, but he managed to raise the rifle and center the crosshairs of the scope on the bull's chest. The old bull stopped just twenty-five human paces away, not quite sure of what he saw. Harvey pulled the trigger. The bullet punched through the bull's brisket, mushrooming to nearly three times its diameter as it plowed through meat and heavy cartilage, to blow away a large portion of the top of his heart. The bull convulsed, dead on his feet. He slowly sank to the ground and was gone.

It was a fast, merciful end to a grand and free life. Hubert gave a loud hoot and slapped Harvey on the back, shocking him out of his mesmerized state. The two men walked quietly over to the dead beast and looked down at his hulking carcass. "Damn," Harvey said. The only man in all of Newfoundland happier than Harvey at that moment was Hubert.

Back up the mountain, we plodded steadily onward and upward. When we came to a cut between two heavily vegetated humps, Cyril noticed a pile of fairly fresh moose dung in the trail. He pointed to it and spoke softly.

"We'll get up on top of this knob and call. This moose can't be too far away."

A few steps farther there was another small rivulet. Cyril unshouldered his pack, reached in and pulled out a large tomato juice can. It had a hole punched in the center of the end which remained, through which there was a long, heavy, cotton shoestring. He made sure all of the string was inside the can, then he bent over and dipped it into the water, shook it around a couple times to wet the string, then dumped it out. He grabbed his ax and pack, and we climbed up the steep side of the knob to our left.

On top of the knob, we had a marvelous view. We crouched down in the scrub. Cyril held the juice can in his left hand and yanked the string through the hole. It produced a raspy, hollow sound, meant to imitate the call of a lovesick moose. He yanked the string three or four times and we waited. A few seconds later, I saw a bit of movement among the scattered spruce trees nearly half a mile away, across the valley before us.

"There's movement," I said quietly, pointing.

We all put our binoculars up and searched the spot. We didn't have to search long though, for a moose promptly popped out of the spruce and came trotting toward us, across the bog valley.

"It's a bull," Cyril said. "You better load up and get yourself ready."

Tom and I continued looking at the moose, trying to size him up.

"I can't be completely sure," Tom said, softly, "but I think it's a young one."

"I think you're right," I said. "I don't see any palms on him."

The bull was now within four hundred yards and closing in on us. I took the binoculars off from around my neck and laid them on my knapsack. Working the bolt on the rifle, I chambered a cartridge, moved forward a couple feet and got into position. The moose stopped in the bottom of the valley below us, in a clump of brush. We could see his head turning in every direction, trying to ascertain just where the call had come from. Cyril cupped his hands to his mouth and grunted twice. The bull's head abruptly snapped in our direction and he began walking up the hill toward us. There were some intervening spruce trees which partially obscured our view of him. When he stepped past them and paused, he was just a little over a hundred yards away, quartering toward us. I put my forward elbow on my left knee, centered the crosshairs on his shoulder and squeezed the trigger. The big rifle barked, the .338 caliber bullet made a supersonic crack as it passed through the air and struck the hapless moose with 4300 deadly foot pounds of energy. The bull staggered and turned the other way. In an instant, I chambered another cartridge and fired again. The bull collapsed and disappeared from sight.

"He's had it," Cyril said.

I turned around, reached out and shook Cyril's hand.

"By God, you're pretty good at this calling."

"Many a bull moose has been killed with an old juice can," he said.

"Congratulations," Tom said, extending his hand.

I shook his hand and was surprised to see that it was trembling. I looked at his face. He looked at me very seriously.

"I can't believe it," he said. "That was the most exhilarating moment I've had in years. Look, my hand is shaking. And you're dead calm."

"Well," I said. "Maybe I have grown a little cold at this. It seems like lifetimes ago since I got excited about killing. With some of us, we kill so that we can hunt . . . Like I said before, the killing is not about sport, it's about eating."

We gathered up our gear and walked down to the moose. He had died in the very unusual and silly looking position of being flat on his back with all four feet in the air. I had a grim and hollow feeling as I stepped up and looked down at him.

"I guess he literally went belly up," I said.

"Yayes, I never seen one end up like that before. The bullets from that big gun must be so heavy they anchored him that way."

"Wow," Tom said. "He's huge. The last time I saw something that big, a cop was sitting on him in Central Park."

Cyril and I laughed.

"I'd reckon he'll weigh a little over nine hundred pounds," I said.

"Yayes, good size, 'bout as big as they gets here. 'Bout three year old I reckon – be fine eatin'."

"Just like whackin' a sophomore looking for a date for the prom . . . Snuffed out in the prime of his life," I said.

"Yayes," Cyril said. "Ya saved the poor lad from a lifetime of heartache with the ladies."

We gutted the moose, so the meat could cool. Cyril cut out the interior fillets and we took them with us back down the mountain.

Hubert and Harvey made it back to camp with the antlers and cape of the old bull just a couple minutes before we arrived. When we came walking up, Harvey was down on one knee with the nearly four-foot-wide antlers in his hands, with Hubert looking on, as Solomon was taking a look at their kill.

"He's a nice one," Sol said.

Tom slapped Harvey on the back.

"All right, Harvey," he yelled.

"Yayes," Cyril said, quietly, "an old bull."

"How can you tell?" Tom asked.

"The way the edges of the palms are rounded like that. A younger bull would have points instead of just these knobs. He's an old bull."

"Had no teeth neither," Hubert said.

We all stood looking at the antlers.

"He was going to be dead in three or four months no matter what," I said. "Congratulations Harvey, you saved the old geezer from a painful, agonizing end."

Harvey couldn't have been soaked with more sweat if he had just run a marathon on an August day, but he was all smiles.

We swapped our hunting stories as we had a very nice lunch of soup and sandwiches. After lunch, Cyril walked out on the porch with a biscuit in his hand and yelled for his pet bird. There were at least four Canada jays flitting about the camp. Cyril held out the biscuit and called, "Here, gik, gik, gik – here gik, gik, gik."

Sure enough, one of the birds flew over and landed on his hand and pecked away at the biscuit.

"Well, I'll – " Tom marveled.

"Somethin', isn't it?" I said.

"Did you raise that bird from a pup, or what?" Tom inquired.

"No," Cyril replied. "He just knows who his friends are. He's an old bird. I don't know where he goes in the winters, but every year when we come back to open the camp for another season he's here with the wife and another brood, lookin' for a handout."

We played around with the jay for a few minutes, then I went over to the cabin to store my binoculars and knapsack. Tom came in and grabbed a very nice looking pair of knee-high rubber boots. He held them in his hand and asked me for my opinion.

"Do you think it would be okay if I gave Cyril my spare boots? Do you think he'd be offended?"

"No, I don't think so," I said. "As a matter of fact, I thought about giving him a pair of mine, but I'm afraid they'd be too big for him. Yours look about right."

"I just wondered what you thought."

"He's a practical man. If you're insistent enough, he'll take 'em."

We went back outside. Cyril was sitting on the bench in front of the kitchen in his bare feet, throwing bread crumbs to the jays.

"Cyril," Tom said, "I would like for you to try on these boots. If they fit you, I'd like for you to keep them."

"Oh, I couldn't take your boots."

"Why not? Yours are destroyed and I have a good pair in reserve."

"Well, then you'd have no dry spares."

"Sure I will," Tom insisted. "I brought three pairs of various types of footwear. I'll be fine. Besides, I'll be out of here in a few days and you'll be stuck here with wet feet. Look, they're brand new. I only bought them because I didn't know what to expect with the terrain here. Once this trip is over, I would probably never wear them again. It would be a waste for them to not get used. I really want you to take them."

Cyril smiled graciously.

"They're fancy camo too. Well, if ya insists, I'll get some dry socks and give 'em a try."

He got up and went inside to get the socks. I smiled at Tom.

"Good sell," I said.

Cyril was back in a minute and sat down and tried the boots. We could see that they were a perfect fit. He stood up and said, "They feels pretty good."

He immediately lost every bit of his accent, as he stuck his thumbs in his belt and started dancing around singing in a deep, country and western voice.

"I've got spurs that jingle, jangle, jingle, as I go ridin' merrily along."

We all laughed at his antics.

He yelled, "Thanks to ya, Tommy. Why I'll be flyin' up the mountain to fetch the meat now, in me new boots. Speakin' of which, I suppose we best get to it. Are ya fellers ready?"

"I am," I said.

Tom nodded.

"Good," Cyril said. He started toward the screened building near the lake shore. "We got the pack frames down here."

"Are ya comin' with us, Harvey?" Hubert asked.

Harvey was sitting on the porch with a can of beer in his hand.

"I've had enough of that mountain. It's your baby now," he said to Hubert. He had the arrogance of a lord talking down to a servant.

The old cook, Solomon gave him a hard look, turned and went into the kitchen. Hubert, Cyril, Tom and I picked up the pack frames and headed off. A short distance from camp, we stopped. Cyril said, "Tommy, you can go with Hubert or us, whichever ya chooses."

"I'll help Hubert," he said.

"Keep your rifle handy," Cyril advised. "Ya never know when you'll come across a moose."

The guides started off in separate directions.

"You're a good man, Tom, to help pack a buddy's meat," I said. "Personally, I wouldn't have a friend like Harvey. A man who won't even help pack out his own meat is one sorry son-of-a-bitch."

We went off in separate directions and spent a long, fly-bitten, laborious afternoon butchering and carrying the moose meat back to the camp. It took two trips for each man to get the job done, and we were loaded heavy both times.

When Cyril and I came stumbling in with the last

load, we were exhausted. Tom was just exiting from the shower building.

"Next," he yelled at us.

"That sounds like a hell of a good idea to me," I said. "Would you like to go first?"

"You go," Cyril said. "I like to wait until after supper."

Harvey had long since showered and was now sitting on the porch with a glass in his hand and about half a bottle of whiskey beside him. I walked up and picked up the bottle.

"By God Harvey," I said, "you may have some redeemin' attributes after all." I looked at the bottle. "Genuine Tullamore Dew, Irish whiskey."

"What is it?" Cyril asked, as he approached.

"It's the best damn whiskey in the world," I said. "You've heard of the good stuff? Well, this is the really good stuff. Next to this, everything else is kerosene."

I tipped the bottle up and took a good drink, then handed it to Cyril.

"Cyril, old boy, may I offer you a drink?"

He accepted the bottle from me and took a good drink.

"Hubert?" he said, handing the bottle up to the old man, who was standing on the porch. Hubert polished off the bottle and handed it back to me. Harvey glanced at us, looking slightly perturbed. I set the bottle back down on the porch and slapped him on the back.

"Don't worry, Harvey," I laughed. "I've got another bottle just like it. We'll break it out shortly."

I went into the cabin and sat down next to the wood stove to take off my boots. Tom was getting dressed.

"Well, did that shower make a new man out of you?" I called.

"Did it ever," he said, sticking his head out of his room. "I can't remember ever appreciating a shower more."

"Nothing like semi-extreme conditions to make a fellow appreciate the simple, little things, is there?"

"No, there isn't."

"Humpin' that moose meat reminds me of an exchange I saw one night in a bar in Red Lodge, Montana years ago. There was this young neophyte from the east pestering this old rancher, pumping him for information on where to go hunting. The old man wasn't paying very much attention to the young dude and barely spoke a word until the dude asked him flat out, 'Where's a good place to shoot a moose?' Well, the old rancher just smiled, took a drink, and said – completely serious and deadpan – 'Next to a pickup truck.'"

Tom laughed.

"That old guy had obviously had some experience moose hunting," he observed.

"Yeah, that's what I thought."

I finished taking off my wet boots and set them

against the wall, behind the stove to dry. Tom came out and sat down to put on his dry shoes.

"I've never worked as hard in my life as I did this afternoon carrying out that meat. And it wasn't nearly as far or as steep as where you shot yours," he said. "It feels good though. This is what I really came here to do. With some food and a good night's sleep, I'll be ready to hit it tomorrow, all over again."

"Well, you'll have ole Cyril's services all to yourself tomorrow. I'll probably sleep in and recoup."

I had gone back to my little room to retrieve a towel and the only bottle of booze I had brought along. Coming back out, I handed the bottle to Tom.

"Here, you better pass this on to Harvey before he blows a gasket. Make sure the other guys get their share, including yourself."

"Thanks."

By the time I emerged from the shower, the sun was setting. I heard an outboard motor and looked out to the lake, where Winston was returning with Ted and Michael. As they approached the shore, Winston killed the motor and they coasted in. Harvey got up and walked halfway to the lake yelling, "Any luck?" I saw heads shaking all around as I ducked into the cabin to finish dressing.

When I came out again, the old cook stuck his head out of the kitchen door and announced, "You fellers all come to supper now."

By then, everyone had concluded marveling at Harvey's antlers and hearing the play by play report on how he had shot it. We all stepped into the kitchen.

"You see anything?" I asked Ted.

"Just a couple caribou," he replied. "You got one though. Congratulations."

He extended his hand.

"Congratulations," Michael said, and I shook his hand as well.

I saw that most of the bottle of my whiskey still remained. I picked it up and poured a good slug into a glass. I held the bottle up and said aloud, "Whiskey!" The bottle was passed around until it had been poured into enough glasses that it was gone. As we sat down, Cyril lifted his glass and stated comically, "Here's to the carybou, the moosybou, and the bearybou."

We chuckled among ourselves and drank to the silly toast.

"Tomorrow," Cyril continued, "Ted, you will go out with Winston. Michael with Hubert, and Tommy and I will go back up the mountain and we'll kill more moose."

We drank and ate with the gusto of hungry, tired men. There was a warm and jovial mood about us, encouraged by the success of the day and the alcohol we had consumed. The subject of moose calling was briefly discussed, which motivated the by now quite drunk, Harvey to stand on the porch calling out the words "oh, moose" in variations of suggestive, feminine voices until we were all near hysteria.

Eventually, Cyril brought out a guitar and sang a couple songs. The second tune he sang was an old mariner's ballad. The lyrics didn't make any particular impression on me until near the end of the song. Cyril played the chord on the old guitar and said, "and here's a verse of me own I wrote just the other night –

The other day the devil came up to old Labrador,
with a shipload of souls from some great tragedy.
He said they came from an island of great despair.
When he first saw it, he stopped and he cursed it right there,
that island in the river by the sea."

As Cyril sang the refrain, I looked at Tom and he at me. It was obvious that he was as curious as I was about the nature of the lyrics. When Cyril had finished the song, Tom questioned him.

"The last verse, the one you wrote yourself, I can't help but be curious about how you came to write such strange lyrics?"

"I don't really know," Cyril answered. "All I know is, I woke up from a sound sleep the other night, I got me flashlight, a pencil and a paper and I wrote it down . . . Remember Winston? Me lad, Winston, he was awoke from some great romance and he asks me what's I'm doin'?"

"I remember," Winston replied.

"What I wants to know is – was she a blonde, a

brunette, or one of them fiery redheads from down at Stephenville that ya was romancin' there Wins?"

We all laughed as Cyril continued.

"To hell with them condoms, just give me that sheet of plywood, ay Winston?"

As we finished laughing, Cyril offered to surrender the guitar to anyone else who wished to perform.

"Does any of you fellers have anything ya wishes to sing?"

"I've got an idea," Michael said.

He stood up and motioned to Ted and Tom, and they huddled for a minute in front of the door. Harvey was too far gone to do anything, but sit and grin. When the three of them turned to face the rest of us, Cyril held up the guitar.

"Thanks," Michael said, "but I think this will be best acappella. Here

goes –"

What followed was a rendition of a long-running skit from the popular TV variety show Hee Haw.

"Up on the mountain and across the bogs,
there are many lonely cow moose looking for Don Juan.
They'd searched and they'd searched and thought they had found him,
but Harvey whacked him, and now he is gone.
Oh where, oh where are you tonight?
You walked away and left me all alone.
I searched the world over and though I'd found true love,
but you met Harvey and pffffthp you were gone."

I laughed harder than I had laughed for a long time. We all thought Harvey would choke to death, the way the laughter got the best of him.

We eventually stumbled out of the kitchen and headed off to bed. As we were leaving Cyril called after us.

"If ya hears somethin' strange when you're tuckin' in, don't come runnin' with rifles a pointin'. It'll just be your old guide Cyril a serenadin' the moose."

We stood scattered about in front of the cabin, hosing down the shrubbery before we retired.

"But you met ole Harvey and pppfffffthp you were gone," I laughed.

"What are you doing to that bush over there, Michael?" Ted yelled.

"Leaving a love letter for the local wolf," he replied.

"There aren't any wolves in Newfoundland," I said.

"Killjoy," Michael yelled.

"It doesn't get better than this," Tom said, looking up at the stars.

"No, I reckon it don't," I said.

"God, I'm enjoying this," Tom elaborated.

"I'd be enjoying myself too if I spent as much time holding onto my dick as you do," Harvey yelled.

We laughed and went into the cabin to turn in for the night. As we were getting undressed and settling in, Michael asked, "What day is it?"

"Monday," Ted called, in reply.

"I mean what day of the month?"

"Who cares, I thought we came out here to forget about shit like that," Ted answered.

"It's Monday, the tenth of September," Tom said. "Why?"

"Some things still operate on a schedule," Michael answered, "like my medication."

Harvey was already snoring.

"Harvey's snoring already?" Tom called out.

"Yeah," Ted said. "I think he's had enough medication already."

Michael had no more than turned out the light when someone shut off the generator and suddenly all was quiet.

Tom lay in his bunk and was given to a sense of great satisfaction. Michael was right, he thought. Back in the city, the world was operating on a bustling, hectic schedule. Tomorrow morning it would be Tuesday, September eleven, 2001. Millions of people would be going to work, and charging off to millions of appointments, and wading through a million endless piles of bullshit. But all he would have to be concerned about was climbing the mountain, enjoying the scenery and camaraderie, and looking for a moose to shoot. It was just that cave man simple. He'd just had one of the very best days of his life and there was the promise that tomorrow might even be better. This was the adventure he had so longed for. He rested so comfortably in his bed, so tired of body and rejuvenated in spirit that it was almost like he was floating. He was overcome with a knowing that all was right in this corner of the world.

Then came the sound of Cyril "serenading the moose." He stood on the porch with a length of rubber hose, swaying and dipping as he blew through it, making a hollow and mournful sound, which called to lovesick moose up and down the valley. No average man could mimic the exact resonance the way Cyril could. The ancient, primeval talent flowed from his throat and spoke to the animals in their own tongue. Time stood still listening to his performance, and the romantic longing of moose was not all that was affected. The ancient spirit in all too modern men was soothed as well.

No sooner had Cyril concluded his serenade, than a murmuring came from across the lake.

"Did you hear that, Homer?" Tom asked, softly.

"Yes," I replied.

"What was it?"

"A loon – a female loon. They often make that sound at night in the late summer and early autumn."

I was very familiar with the various calls of loons. There was a pair which nested on the lake where I lived back home. Their late summer call was like no other sound in the world and it affected me deeply. The voices of the animals – the mating call of the moose, the late summer moaning, murmur of the loon – like the various other utterances of nature, spoke with yearning and emotion. They were sometimes all too universal.

Many times on late August nights when it was warm and the windows were open, I was awakened in the wee hours of the morning from far off dreams of times long gone by. The sound came through the mist, over the surface of the water from an unseen place, ever haunting, plaintive – like the voice of a lover lost eons ago, eternally calling for her mate. Tom didn't have my experience with loons, but the sound of the call had the same deeply emotional effect on him. He thought of his wife, so far away from him, so alone, so vulnerable. She was the only part of his familiar, far removed world which he missed. The voice of the loon humbled him with a longing.

CHAPTER FIVE

When I was rudely jolted awake the next morning by the sound of the generator starting up, I smiled with the warm satisfaction of a hunter who had already killed his moose, and I rolled over and went back to sleep. I tuned out the sounds of Michael, Ted and Tom clamoring to get dressed and heading off to breakfast, for an early start to another day's hunting. Sometime later, I was awakened again by the cessation of Harvey's snoring. The sun was well up and shining through the little window above the bunk. As I was getting dressed, Harvey regained consciousness. He was utterly incommunicative, which suited me just fine the first thing in the morning.

We proceeded over to the kitchen, and discovered, as expected, that everyone else had long since departed. Old Sol graciously chided us for our laziness, then served us a fine breakfast of pancakes and sausage.

Up the mountain, at that moment, Cyril and Tom

paused at the edge of Wet Ass Hill. The pet jay came flitting along and landed on Cyril's hat.

"There ya be again, ya little beggar," Cyril chided. He reached up with his right hand and the bird stepped onto his finger. Cyril held the jay at nearly arm's length and talked to him again. "I got no biscuit for ya now. Ya has to go back to camp and leave us to our business . . . Go on, go back."

Just as if he completely understood what Cyril had said to him, the jay flew away, down the mountain, in the direction of the camp. Tom was amazed. The relationship between Cyril and the jay was a simple little thing, almost an inconsequential part of their everyday lives for years now. But to a man like Tom Coach it was the substance of dreams, or a fairy tale.

They slogged across the boggy expanse of Wet Ass Hill and quietly up the mountain for nearly two hours, before they stopped for a break. There was an outcropping, from where one had a commanding view of a wide expanse of the country in three directions. Cyril took off the pack frame he carried and sat down on a rock.

"We'll take a rest here for a while and give a good look around with our bifocals."

Tom dumped the pack from his shoulders and sat down on another rock about six feet away from Cyril. He pulled out his binoculars and started scanning the country below them in all directions for sign of a moose.

"How long have you been guiding here?" Tom asked.

"Let's see . . . About twenty-five year, I reckon."

"Wow, twenty-five years, right here, in this same place?"

"Yayes. It's been so long, I could walk up this trail in the dark."

They were quiet for a moment as they scanned the country with their field glasses.

"She don't look much like New York City, does she?" Cyril mused.

"No, it certainly doesn't."

"Ya ever see anything like this before?"

"No, not quite like this. It's unique country . . . Beautiful and unique . . . I'm really enjoying this whole experience."

"When ya gets back home, the wife won't know what ta do with ya, ay?"

"That's a possibility," Tom conceded.

"Is she a good woman, your wife?"

It seemed like an almost impertinent question, Tom thought, but there was no harm in being honest. It was, after all, an easy question to answer.

"She's the best," Tom answered. "A man couldn't do better . . . Oh, we've had our difficulties over the years – all the stress with the kids and work, but if I went back in time and had the chance to make the choices of a young man, I'd marry her all over again."

"That good, ay . . . Ya has children, ay?"

"Yes, a daughter, thirteen and a son, ten. You?"

"Yayes . . . I has a son. He's about twenty-eight, I think – lives down in Ontario. He's a family of his own and a good job. I has a daughter – near twenty-three. She just graduates from the technical college last spring. She works with the computers – lives in an apartment in Corner Brook."

"And you and your wife?"

"We lives in a little village up the north coast. We were born and raised there, but the children, they don't stay. There's no money there for them . . . I went away too for a while when I was younger."

After some silence as they continued looking around with their binoculars, Tom asked, "Where did you go – when you were younger – when you went away?"

"Oh, I went to Alberta and works in the oil fields out there. Then I was on a ship for a while."

"In the merchant marine?"

Cyril thought for a moment, then replied.

"Yayes . . . But I doesn't want to go away no more. There's not much money where I lives, but I fishes and traps lobster and crabs in the summer, and I guides you fellers and traps in the fall, and we gets by . . . It's makin' a livin' in the old ways. But it gets harder to do, and poorer as it goes. The children, they don't want to be poor, so they goes away."

Tom understood what he was talking about.

"What about you, Tommy? Has ya lived in the city all your life?"

"No," Tom answered slowly. "I was raised in a little

town in Vermont. Like where you live, it was a place that was poor. I was one of the children who went away."

"Hm," Cyril mused.

"I met my wife, Barbara, in college. She was from New York. When we graduated, she went to work for her father's investment firm making fairly serious money. I figured I could teach anywhere, so I followed her to New York. We've been married and I've been at Columbia University for twenty years now."

"And your wife?"

"She's a stock analyst now. Her father died a couple years ago and left her a substantial holding in the company . . . The stress of the job has been taking a real toll on her though, and us. If I could convince her to sell out and quit, I'd like to take our investments and move out to the country. I could teach at some small college and she could do whatever, and we could finish raising our kids in a better environment . . . But I don't know if it will ever happen . . . Lately, I've come to have a lot of respect, and in some ways envy, for guys like you and Homer, who stayed and managed to make a living where you were raised. It's a more natural, more compatible life."

"She's mighty poor, though."

"Yes," Tom replied. "I think the money has a way of humbling us all in some fashion."

They were quiet for a while, steadily glassing the

distant landscape. Finally, Cyril lowered his field glasses to rest his shoulders.

"Ya know, the old couple who left when yous came in the other day – they was interestin' folks – fine people. One afternoon see, the one couple they was out with Hubert and Winston. So the only ones in camp was me and Sol, and the other couple and they was all takin' a nap after lunch. Old Sol, he was a snorin'. I goes out to the outhouse and when I comes back past the cabin, I hears the old couple a goin' to it inside. And from the sound of it, she was enjoyin' it plenty. I smiles to meself and went on about me business. The next day, we be up here like this, me and the old gentleman, and I asks him how old they was. He says he's sixty-eight and the wife was seventy. Been married forty-six year. I thought it was... bein' together all that time..."

"Inspiring – inspirational?"

"Yayes." Cyril paused for a moment. "Havin' a good woman, and some family – I think it's what really matters, ay?"

Yes, Tom thought, it was what mattered. Those kind of basics in life were easy to lose sight of, though. In New York it was really easy.

He was just starting to reflect on his life when Cyril announced, "I sees your moose."

Tom turned around to see where Cyril was looking with his binoculars.

"Where?"

"Way over there, on the edge of the bog."

Tom focused on the area.

"He's a nice bull," Cyril said. "I thinks we better go get him."

Back at the camp, in the late morning there were only Sol, Harvey and I lazily going about the business of keeping from being bored. Harvey was engaged in what appeared to be his favorite pastime, sitting on the porch drinking a beer. He appeared to be a man who was very much out of his element. Back in New York, his money and business expertise gained him respect from those around him. Whether he was at his office, home, or some social setting, he was recognized and given deference by people similar to him. He was so used to things being that way that he had gained an ego of considerable proportions. However, here in the wilderness, to guys like Sol and me, he was just a city-slicker doofus who couldn't do justice to his spiffy L. L. Bean wardrobe. Among his own crowd, he was a man of almost comic good humor, but we had seen that side of him only very sporadically, when he had too much to drink. Social superiority is only acceptable when the peasants concede to be lorded over. Sol and I were not deferring types. We treated Harvey as an equal and that wasn't just quite acceptable to him. I walked out of the cabin with my knife and a stone and sat down on the bench in front of the kitchen. As I started to sharpen the blade, I thought I would make some attempt at conversation with Harvey.

"What do you do back in New York, Harvey?"

He was unresponsive to the point of acting like he hadn't heard me. The slight annoyed me somewhat.

"Got a porch there where you sit and drink beer all day?"

"Investment banker," he said, finally.

"What exactly does an investment banker do," I asked.

Solomon came out of the kitchen and leaned in the doorway.

"I find investments for my bank," Harvey replied, in a tone which indicated that any moron would, of course, know that.

"She pays pretty good, ay?" Sol asked.

"I do all right," Harvey said.

"How about yous, Homer? What does ya do back at your home?"

"I've got a little logging outfit," I said.

"A logger – she's a mighty hard work, ay."

"Yeah, some days lately I think I'm starting to get a little gray in the whiskers for it."

"She pays okay, though?" Sol asked.

"No," I said. "It's getting to be a pretty poor way to make a living. But I've been doing it most of my adult life. I'm good at it and I like doing it. I reckon until I publish a best-seller, or get squashed like a bug from a big tree falling on me, I'll probably keep on doing it."

"Ya writes too, does ya?"

"Yeah," I said. "I've got no more sense. That's one of the things I like about logging. It gives me the freedom to spend a few days in the winter, when it's really cold outside, to sit at my desk, uninterrupted and write. Granted, I've been at it for over thirty years, off and on, and haven't made a nickel at it yet, but it's important."

I had finally tweaked Harvey's interest.

"Why in the world," he railed, "would anybody fuck around for thirty years at something that you never make any money at?"

"Why indeed?" I smiled at old Sol. "I'll bet you never did a single thing in your whole life that you didn't get paid for, did you Harvey?"

Apparently one little blurt was all he would condescend to. He just blew air through his teeth and looked away.

"You see Harvey, it's an altruistic thing. That, and I've got a problem with obsession and the urge to get things properly said, so that guys like you don't have the last word on everything . . . I expect about fifty years after I've been shot through the head by some twenty-first century Gestapo officer, some techno genius will figure out how to open my gun safe without being blown to smithereens from all the booby traps I've got in there. He'll fish out all the original copies of my manuscripts, and in the wonderfully clear hindsight of history, he'll realize – gee this guy was a genius. So, long after everybody I know is dead and gone, somebody I never knew will become rich and I'll finally be famous. That's the realistic, lofty goal I aspire to."

The old cook laughed and went back into the kitchen. Harvey just looked away and was utterly unresponsive. Men like Sol and I were beneath him. He had so much disdain for me, he couldn't even manage a sense of humor.

I was finishing working on the knife, a while later, when Sol came to the door and said, "I don't think any of the other boys are coming in for lunch. We'll eat a little now, if ya fellers wants."

He had no more than said it, when we looked up and saw Cyril and Tom coming in, carrying a set of antlers and a load of meat.

"By God, you got one," I yelled.

Harvey jumped up and walked out to meet them.

"Way to go, buddy," he yelled.

Cyril was hanging the meat in the screened shed as Tom slipped out of his pack frame and let the antlers slide to the ground.

"Another old bull," I observed.

"Yes," Tom said, "like yours, Harvey, he didn't have any teeth left."

"It sort of begs the question," I said. "Are you fellows really engaged in hunting, or euthanasia?"

They laughed.

We listened to Tom and Cyril tell about how they had gotten the moose, while we had a leisurely lunch. They rested for a bit afterwards. While we were sitting around on the porch yucking it up, Angus, the man who owned the outfitting operation, landed on the lake with his single-engine Cessna. He was a very congenial man, but didn't stay or talk very long, as he was on a tight schedule. We loaded up the moose meat we had accumulated in the screened shed, and he took off.

We watched the small float plane lift off the water and ascend skyward.

"Well, I suppose we had best go fetch the rest of the meat," Cyril said.

"Could you get it all in one trip with three men hauling?" I asked.

"Yayes," Cyril replied.

"Then I'll go with you," I said.

"Thanks, Homer," Tom said. "That's generous of you."

"I've got nothing better to do."

We picked up the pack frames and started off.

"You're not taking your rifle?" I asked Tom. He looked at me with mine firmly in hand and was a bit perplexed.

"Well, no," he replied. "Should I?"

"Spoken by a man who obviously never had a difference of opinion with a bear over a chunk of dead meat," I said.

He stopped, momentarily considering that prospect.

"Ah, don't worry about it. I've got mine. We'll be all right. Ninety percent of the time, bears won't find a carcass until a week later."

We started off again, after Cyril. A couple minutes later, Tom spoke as we trudged across the bog.

"I've got a philosophical question for you," he said.
"Yeah?"
"If a bear shit in the forest and there was no one there to smell it, would it still stink?"

I chuckled a little as we continued on our way. It was obvious Tom was enjoying himself immensely.

It was a fine afternoon. Tom and I were positively aglow with our hunting success as was Cyril for his role in it. In other reaches of the forested mountainside, Ted and Michael were in that phase of high anticipation with their guides as everyone enjoyed the favorable weather.

When afternoon merged into evening, Harvey was napping in his bunk completely oblivious to everything. The old cook, Solomon, was leisurely preparing the supper feast when it suddenly occurred to him that it was time to turn on the radio for the weather report and the news. He turned on the switch and mere seconds passed before the incoherent static gave way to the news. And the news was not the usual inconsequential blather. Even though it spoke of events far away, it stunned him. Suddenly, he realized that there were men in the camp to whom this particular news would literally be a matter of life and death. He grabbed his reading glasses, a pen and a scrap of paper, and sat down to scribble some hasty notes. When the blurb had passed, he lay down the pen, took off his glasses and ran his hand over his bald head. He stared straight ahead, out the open door, at the softening sunshine on the placid lake and wondered how he was going to break it to the men when they came in.

Tom had shot his moose considerably farther away than I had. The sun was beginning to set and we were growing leg weary as we descended toward the final stretch to camp. It wasn't hard for me to tell that Tom was especially tired. The exhaustion didn't dampen his enthusiasm, however. We encountered Michael and Hubert a couple hundred yards from camp.

"Did you get one?" Michael yelled.

"He sure did," I yelled back.

Tom was positively beaming with pride and satisfaction. We closed upon each other and formed a single line as we chattered and made our way toward the camp. We heard the sound of the outboard motor and saw Ted and Winston approaching in one of the boats. They came coasting in to the shore just as we were slipping out of the pack frames next to the meat shed.

"Wow," Tom said, straightening back up after dumping the pack. "It really feels good to be able to set that down."

"It sure does," I said, "and I only went up the mountain once today. Your ass has got to be draggin'."

"It sure is," Tom replied.

But he was all smiles. I couldn't help but think that it had to be one of the best days of his life. I had never seen a man more tired and yet more alive than he was at that moment. Harvey came stumbling out of the cabin, having been awakened by the noise and came down to join in the revelry. We were all happy and looking forward to the relaxation of the evening. We hung the meat in the screened shed, splashed off our hands and faces in the water beside the dock, and headed for the kitchen, where we knew a fine supper was waiting for us.

I was the first one through the kitchen door.

"Sol, I – "

There are no secrets between like men. The look on the old man's face froze me in the middle of words I had already forgotten. Something was wrong in a major way. As the rest of the men filed in past me, I felt myself being pulled away to some distant post of observation. Whether it was old Sol's countenance or my reaction to it I do not know, but one by one the men stopped their chatter and looked at the old man.

He stood with a scrap of paper in one hand and his glasses in the other. When the entire room was dead quiet, he began.

"Everyone is here, yes? There was news, come a while ago on the radio. I only want to say it once." He put on his glasses and held up the piece of paper to the light. He knew what the news was. He had mentally rehearsed just how he would tell it several times, but it was easier to look at the scrap of paper than at the faces of the men he had to tell it to.

"This morning, in what they says appears to be

a carefully coordinated attack, there was four commercial airliners hijacked shortly after takeoff from the airports in New York and Boston. The planes they were commandeered, then they was flown by men who they believes to be middle-eastern, Islamic terrorists. One of the planes, she was intentionally flown into one of the towers of the World Trade Center in New York where it immediately burst into a large fire. A few minutes later, a second plane she crashes into the other tower of the Trade Center. Both towers they are collapsed, and the whole Trade Center is destroyed. A while later, a third plane she crashes into the Pentagon building in Washington, D.C. The fourth plane, it crashed in a field in Pennsylvania after some of the passengers they fought with the hijackers for control of the plane. In Washington, the dead are feared to number over six hundred. All are dead aboard the plane which crashed in Pennsylvania. And in New York, they says there are thousands are known to be dead. Officials cannot give a figure for the death and injured toll because so many they are unaccounted for."

Tom had slowly sunk into a chair and put his face in his hands. Harvey abruptly sat down, reached for the bottle on the table, and poured himself a stiff drink.

"Both of their wives worked at the World Trade Center," Michael said to the rest of us.

Solomon took off his glasses. His face was long as

he looked at the two men. I glanced at Cyril. Even a character like him was at a loss. Like the rest of us, his eyes were wide open with the look of a man who absolutely did not know what to say.

The conspiracy had finally emerged, and had just landed a hard blow. I felt like I had just been kicked in the gut, and I didn't even know anyone who lived in New York. I looked down at Tom. In all my life, I had never seen a man fall emotionally from a higher point to a lower one. It was like he had just plunged off a thousand-foot cliff and was now hovering somewhere a few feet above the rocks below. We all cringed at the thought of seeing him splatter.

Tom stood up abruptly and walked outside. He went halfway to the lake and just stood there with his back to us, looking out over the water. I turned slightly and looked at Harvey. He was doing what he seemed to do best, which was sucking down alcohol.

I looked at the bottle he was pouring from. *Vodka, I thought, the man is sucking down vodka.* In the three days we had been there, I had seen him drink brandy, gin, scotch, whiskey, and now vodka. As far as I was concerned, there was no hope for finding a backbone in a man who couldn't even demonstrate a preference for a type of liquor.

Tom came walking back in just as abruptly as he had left a minute and a half before. His mind and emotions were no doubt racing a mile a minute, but his face was stoic.

"Michael," he said. "Can I use your cell phone?"

"Of course. I'll get it."

Michael went for the phone and was back with it in half a minute's time. He handed it to Tom on the porch. We were all still speechless as Tom took a deep breath and punched in the number. Every man waited for a response, but there was none. Tom lowered the phone and said, "there's no service. It's dead."

"It won't work down here in the valley," Cyril said. "The only place you can get a signal is from the top of the mountain."

Tom turned and paced to the end of the porch. After a moment, he turned to Cyril.

"You said this morning you were so familiar with the trail up the mountain that you could climb it in the dark. Could you take me to the top of the mountain where this thing will get a signal? Would you?"

He looked Cyril straight in the eye. Cyril was solemn. He appreciated just what was being asked of him. It would be no small endeavor to climb the mountain at night, but he well understood why the request was made.

"I've never actually done it, but I believes I could. If you're of a mind to give it a go, I'll do it."

"Thanks," Tom said. "How soon?"

"Now," Cyril replied. "If we leaves right now, we may be able to get past Wet Ass Hill before it is completely dark. Get your raincoat and a hat. The weather may turn rough later on."

Tom hurried off toward the cabin to get his coat. Cyril nodded to Solomon as he went into the back room. The old cook cut a couple thick slices off the roast he had made for supper and made a pair of big sandwiches. Cyril came out with his coat, shoving the camp cell phone in his pocket.

"We takes this one too, just in case."

He was chugging a glass of orange juice when Tom came back, ready to go. Cyril looked at Tom, then reached behind the door and retrieved an implement which he handed to him.

"A feller left this here a couple year back. He said it was a climbing pick. Don't lose it. It may be a good thing to have in your hand if ya takes a slide or runs into an ornery critter in the dark."

Cyril picked up one of the big beefy sandwiches and grabbed his ax. Solomon handed the other sandwich toward Tom.

"No thanks," Tom said. "I really can't eat anything."

Without hesitation, Cyril tucked the ax under his arm grabbed the sandwich and strode out the door with a sandwich in each hand.

"Good luck." Ted slapped Tom on the back.

"Yeah, good luck," Michael said.

Tom paused briefly at the door and looked down at Harvey. He merely sat staring straight ahead, and was completely unresponsive. Tom sighed and walked out the door.

I was standing on the porch. Tom turned his face to me as he passed.

"You keep your mind on what you're doing up there – especially around those tubs," I said.

"Sounds like good advice," Tom replied as he went down the steps.

Sol came out on the porch and called after them.

"We'll keep the generator running and the lights on, so ya has something to steer by."

We watched as they disappeared behind the spruce trees beside the meat shed.

"They're in for one rough night," I said, stepping into the kitchen.

"Yes they are," Ted added. "If I was in Tom's shoes though, I'd have to know too."

"It's a damn risky thing to do if you ask me," Michael said. He was clearly not too happy about it. "I just hope it doesn't turn into yet another tragedy."

We all sat down and ate, though it was not with the usual gusto. The talk was muted and sparse. The mood was affected as much by the tedious presence of Harvey as much as by the news of the tragedy itself. His arrogant streak seemed to broaden, as though the source of his affliction was from having to suffer the company of the rest of us in his time of trial. I tried to ratchet up some measure of compassion for the man, but it was difficult.

On the trail up the mountain, it was quiet. Despite being busily engaged with munching the sandwiches, Cyril made fast, long strides. He was a damn tough man, Tom thought – and a good man too. He had every confidence that he'd get him to the top of the mountain, darkness be damned. It was what he would learn when he got to the top that truly had him worried. My God, what was he going to do if Barbara was gone? He didn't want to think about it. He refused to think about it. He wasn't even going to prepare himself for that option. But he had to know; as soon as possible he had to know. *Don't even think about it,* he told himself. *Just get to the top and find out.* There wasn't even good reason to hope or pray for a favorable outcome to what had happened. It was hours past. It had already been decided. He had had no input of any kind in the situation and he had no control of it now. It had already been decided without him, and there wasn't a damn thing he could do about it. All he could do was to get to the top and find out. Either she was dead or she was alive.

Then, with the horrific suddenness of a lightning bolt, another possibility occurred to him. What if she was injured, or crippled, or barely clinging to life longing to see him. Or worse yet, what if she was buried in the rubble, trapped, mutilated and all alone. And here he was a thousand miles away, of no aid or comfort to her or their children. Lord, he was so far away, so utterly useless to them. It was driving him to madness thinking about it. Nothing was worse than not knowing. He had to get to the top to find out.

At the edge of the soggy, open expanse of Wet Ass

Hill, Cyril stopped and turned to him. The sun was long gone and the dim light was fading fast.

"I know ya has a thousand things in your mind, but keep a clear head and mind your step. Ya be no good to anyone drowned and lost in one of the pools."

Tom reached into his coat pocket and pulled out a small flashlight.

"No don't use the light. I've got one here too," Cyril said, patting his coat pocket. "But if we starts using them now we'll be lost. Besides, the batteries may not last all the way up and back down. Ya stays two steps behind me and force your eyes to see. Hold tight to the pick. If ya slips and falls, ya hammer it into the ground to stop yourself."

Cyril turned and started off again, and Tom followed, two steps behind, just as he had been instructed. *Pay attention,* he told himself. *Don't let everybody down by screwing up. Focus on what you're doing. Don't be such a dumb-ass, city slicker. Cyril wouldn't have to tell Homer what to do here. He shouldn't have to tell you either,* he told himself. *And the last thing he should have to do is fish your soggy ass out of one of the bathtubs.* Besides, he thought, if he fell and got hurt, he would never make it to the top. He wouldn't find out what he so desperately needed to know. He followed two steps behind Cyril, he watched where he placed his feet, and he forced his eyes to see and his feet to feel for the grip.

In due course, they passed the dangerous stretch and got on more solid ground. Tom's mind was overloaded, spinning through an endless maze of possibilities which he feared. He couldn't help himself. He began to become numbed inward. His body went on autopilot, trudging through the growing darkness, following the sound of the guide's footsteps.

Back in camp, things were pretty quiet. We had finished our supper. Hubert was in the back room rolling cigarettes and talking with Winston. Solomon was fiddling around with the dishes. I was sitting at one end of the long table with a glass of water and Harvey was at the other end with what was left of a bottle of Vodka. Michael was sitting beside the open door with a beer, and Ted was against the wall, in the middle of the table. No one had said anything of substance for quite a while. I tried not to look at Harvey. I had a sense that he was becoming agitated. The pressure of the situation and the influence of the booze was making him itch for a fight.

I glanced at him to see that he was staring straight at me. When my eyes met his, he blurted out, "I'm surprised you're not out dancing on the porch. After all, you must be feeling smug as hell. Now you can claim to the whole world that your cockamamie prediction came true."

I gave him a hard look.

"You're out of line, Harvey," Ted said.

"Just because I saw it coming, doesn't mean I wanted it to happen," I said. "I expect there will be plenty of barbarians in the world who will be dancing in the streets over this, though."

Harvey looked away, took a drink, and resumed his silent brooding. Yeah, I thought, he was sure a hard man to have compassion for. Nevertheless, I controlled myself. I was cutting him some slack over the possibility of his wife being dead, but a remark like that came perilously close to deserving an ass kicking.

We resumed our quiet vigil, collectively uncomfortable with knowing what Tom and Cyril must be going through, and individually tortured with our own thoughts of anxiety and what was transpiring beyond our control, a thousand miles away.

Poor Michael was ridden with guilt. He was a paramedic. He was consumed with horrific visions of the devastation and the hundreds of injured that there surely must be. He was certain he was needed at home and he was not there. He had deserted his post to go off on this lark. He was a sensitive and caring man. It was as though a bottle of acid had been poured on his conscience and was steadily burning a hole through it. In his mind, he could hear the cries and see the suffering, and he was not there.

Ted was sifting through evidence in his mind. Just who the hell had done this, and why? If Homer was right about this, he thought – and he probably was – we were all in deep shit and there was probably even deeper shit to come. It was going to take a lot of investigation to get to the bottom of this. Would it truly be allowed to be done, or had all the conclusions already been scripted? Would the people at the top of the organization which was truly responsible for this attack really be brought to justice, or would they be allowed to get away as was so often the case? Unlike Michael, he felt no guilt about not being home, and he did not wish to be there now. He only wished he knew more and had more influence to do something about it. It didn't matter if he was in New York or on vacation in Newfoundland, he was too ignorant and too powerless.

Harvey's mind was a muddle of various emotions, few of which could be easily understood or found acceptable by most men. He would feign deep concern over his wife, but it was not honest. If she was dead, some uncomfortable, inconvenient adjustment would be required, but he would collect the life insurance and inherit her share of their jointly-held property, and he would go on. The thought of losing her had never really been unacceptable to him. There were other women in the world, some of them prettier than the woman he had married and fattened into middle age. He was concerned about his business. He felt the bank would probably be better off if he was at his desk instead of sitting on his drunken ass in the boonies. But hey, there were benefits to being away right now. It was a cinch that the financial world was going to be in total freakin' chaos. Hard, fast decisions were going to have to be made, and heads would eventually roll if the wrong decisions were made. He didn't have anything to worry about. He wasn't there. He couldn't possibly be held responsible.

The thing that really tormented Harvey was what he envisioned as a loss of control. He liked to have everything nailed down. He preferred to believe that his money and influence could insure affluence and security. Beyond that, he had long had his beliefs and politics filed away in some comfortable, preconceived slots. If that asshole Homer was really right, everything he believed and stood for was turned upside down. If the real enemy wasn't the goddamn Republicans and the SEC do-gooders, a whole can of worms that he didn't even want to look at was opened. His sense of security and his world view had taken a very serious hit. It was unacceptable to him – it just couldn't be.

As for me, I didn't think about any of the things the others bothered themselves with. My own problem was that my world view was of a picture so vast and all-encompassing that I was constantly at odds, failing to break it down into small enough detail to work constructively with it. It did not seem to matter that knowledge was so clear and patterns were so familiar that I could constantly predict what would happen, because I was ever without influence and helpless to stop anything, and I was beggared by cynicism.

For two months, I had waited for the shoe to drop, wondering on a daily basis what form the attack would take and where it would hit. Never, in my wildest dreams, had I envisioned that when it came I would find myself sitting beside men directly affected by it. It made the experience a great deal more abrupt and personal than I had imagined it would be. I thought about my friend, Ed, and the extended conversation we had had a couple months earlier where he had predicted that something like this would soon happen. Ed had nailed it with an uncanny precision. He was an airline pilot. Several years before, when he had been between jobs, he had spent several months as a flight instructor. Before our meeting in July, one of his old flight instructor acquaintances had told him of concerns he'd had about the number of semi-shiftless middle-eastern types who were enrolled in flight schools around the country. Ed – good, old, ever-seeking-the-facts, Ed, had made a sufficient number of inquiries into what was going on, that he had become convinced that either Arab terrorists had a plan to commandeer commercial airliners and use them in an attack, or they would become the carefully made patsies for such an attack. When he had told me about it, even I had thought it was so far-fetched that I never followed up on it, or even mentioned it to many others. I knew half a dozen guys like Ed; men employed by the FBI or government intelligence agencies, or in jobs that frequently took them to far corners of the globe; men who were keenly observant and concerned with the truth, who sometimes shared information and insights with me. They were, collectively, my own little, personal intelligence agency. My liaisons with them were frequently very secretive affairs, and a couple times in the past they had proven to be extremely useful to me. But what the hell had we accomplished this time? Ed had known exactly what was coming down, but was powerless to stop it. Hell, he hadn't even been able to conclusively persuade me. Had I been too smug? Was I to some degree, in my own way, as blind as everyone else, or was there just too damned much information to comb through and make sense of? And what could I have done anyway? I had never felt so powerless in my life. I wondered how many thousand other obscure, small-time paranoids were out there with their eyes and ears wide open, quietly gathering data in this information age; good men, objectively cognizant of what dangers lurked in the machinations around them, who were just as utterly helpless to stop the evil.

I thought about all the implications of what had happened and all that would surely come because of it. I was right about New York City being the new Rome. It was the seat of power over an empire more vast and influential than anything the old Romans of two thousand years ago could have imagined, and just as rotten to the core with perversity and corruption as any powerful city-state had ever been. Like the old Rome, it was a place glorious only to Romans. There were, to be sure, plenty of non-Romans who viewed the city with a sense of awe, but mostly the rest of the world looked upon it with either indifference or hatred. Sumer, Ninevah, Rome, Tenochtitlán, New York; the history of mankind was the story of the progression from one dominant sphere of influence to the next, each one reaching further than the one before. It was an unfortunate cycle, which seemingly could not be broken.

I looked back through the ages, through the haze of the many centuries which had passed, to a pitched, shrill battle on an otherwise fine summer afternoon. I saw a rag-tag army of Picts and Scots engaged in a desperate fight against the Roman legions in the shadow of Hadrian's Wall. A vision of horror was burned into my very DNA of the clan from which I was descended lying naked, bloody and dead in the bright sun. I sat there with my balding head and my graying red beard, thinking who would ever have thought, all those eons ago, that one day the very image of a pure bred ancient Celt would be born in a province of the great empire, owing allegiance to Rome.

And there I sat, lost in the contemplation of all which had transpired. In my mind, I could see Ed

Novak, dressed in his pilot uniform with his officer's hat on his head, lifting his face to scrutinize the strange bit of technology on the fuselage of the jet airliner. I could see the squint of his eye and feel the questions which percolated through his mind. I could see the plane flying like a deadly missile, possibly without even a single human on board, toward the distant skyscraper. I could see the turret on the bottom of the cockpit; the workings gyrating and making adjustments until it collided with the building. I wondered if there was some unfortunate soul who looked up from his or her desk at that last fraction of a second to the horror of the thing plowing them into eternity. The impact, the inexorable explosion, the fire, the death, the shock, the injury, the pandemonium, the terror – I wondered if any of it registered with the one who stood up from the console which had remotely flown the monstrous weapon, or if the undoubtedly huge sum of money which was probably handed to him in a duffle bag, was the real reason why he did the awful deed. I could see the hordes fleeing for their lives and the firemen, who were surely there, spending themselves heroically in a battle against impossible odds. And, somewhere a safe distance away, someone was, no doubt, smugly celebrating the success of what he had wrought.

 We had been sitting very quietly for a long time. Finally, the old cook asked, "Does ya think there will be war?"

Harvey never moved, or gave any indication at all that he had even heard the question. Ted and Michael looked up, but neither offered a response. It was rude to the old man to not answer, so finally I said, "It's a surety there will be war. It's part of the plan, and I expect that years from now, most people will remember this as the day when it started."

Harvey glared at me from the other end of the table. He had the look of a man looking for any excuse for a fight.

"I take it by the way you said that, that you don't think this is a legitimate Pearl Harbor type day."

"Oh, it's a legitimate Pearl Harbor type day all right. And the only reasonable recourse is to systematically hunt down every last son-of-a-bitch responsible for it and kill 'em. And I mean every last son-of-a-bitch who had a hand in it, from the lowest level operative, to the uppermost scheming, duplicitous, demonic bastard . . . But you're right, for guys like me, this whole sordid, all-encompassing conflict started on April 19, 1993."

"What the fuck has that got to do with anything?" Harvey blurted out contemptuously.

"That was the day the feds burned down the Branch Davidian compound at Waco," Ted offered.

"I'm glad the feds torched those mother-fuckers," Harvey yelled. "Personally, I think the lunatic mothers torched themselves, but if the feds did it, I'm good with that. No good was going to come from those mother-fucking lunatic, subversive cocksuckers. If we didn't learn anything else today, I think we should have learned that it's preferable to strike those kind of assholes before they strike us!"

He had worked himself into an absolute furor. Even his New York friends were eyeing him incredulously.

Personally, I had had a belly full of him for three days, and now he was sorely trying me.

He glared at me with an insane intensity and continued his rant.

"If you want to know what I think the real tragedy of that Waco thing was – I think it was that the rest of the subversive, mother-fuckin', conspiracy theory nutcases, like you, weren't in the place to get fried with 'em."

I glared back at him. There were a great many things I could have said, but my temper had flared well past the point of anything approaching eloquent articulation. I slammed my hands on the table, ready to launch out of my chair, and lambasted him back.

"A communist, moron, asswipe like you has a lot of damn nerve calling me unpatriotic or subversive. You're living proof that what Pete Day said is right – with enough education, you can cure ignorance, but there's no hope for stupidity."

Just then, Harvey glanced to the side, and a jolt, like an electrical shock, went through me as I realized what he was about to do. Michael, who had not yet shot a moose, had leaned his rifle beside the door where it would be handy. The bolt was open and the chamber was empty, but the magazine was loaded. At that very moment, there wasn't a doubt in my mind that Harvey was going for it, and he was crazy enough to use it.

In a sudden explosion of movement, we both jumped up simultaneously. Harvey went for the rifle, and I went for him. He grabbed the gun and slammed the bolt shut, chambering a live cartridge. I bounded across the room with fast, giant steps and grabbed the forearm of the rifle with my right hand, shoving it upward and at an angle away from me. As the muzzle swung towards him, Ted dove under the table. The rifle went off with a deafening blast and blew a hole through the wall just above where Ted's head had been an instant earlier. I clamped my hands firmly on the gun and struggled with Harvey. The fat man outweighed me by over fifty pounds, but he didn't spend his days muscling a chainsaw through hardwood logs. I stepped on his foot and shoved him backward through the open door, wrenching the rifle from him and smacking him in the face with the flat side of the buttstock, all in one big, sweeping movement. He went flying across the narrow porch and sprawling down the steps.

"That's just like a gun control advocate, to go for a gun the minute things go south," I yelled.

I swung the rifle by the barrel and whacked it on the edge of the porch, breaking the stock off of it.

"That's my . . . rifle," Michael moaned, as I whacked it again and bent the barrel, rendering it useless.

Harvey was on his hand and knees, trying to get to his feet. I pitched the remains of the rifle onto the ground and leapt off the porch, booting Harvey in the rear end as I did so. He was knocked flat on his face, but bounced back up and tried frantically to flee on his hands and knees. Everyone poured out of the kitchen door behind me, as I chased him toward the lake and booted him again. As he bounced back up again, I grabbed him by the back of the neck and the seat of the pants and got him going with enough momentum to pitch him into the lake. He hit the dark, cold water with an enormous splash. I immediately waded in after him. Standing in water just over my knees, I grabbed him by the neck and shoved his head under the water. He choked and thrashed as Michael stood on the shore and yelled at me.

"You're killing him."

"I believe that's what he had in mind for me."

"He's just drunk and confused."

"Well I'm not confused," I yelled back at Michael. I turned back to Harvey as I continued forcing him under. "In another life, I would kill you."

I hoisted his head out of the water and bellowed at him as he choked and sputtered.

"What we're gonna do here Harvey, is sober you up, and then you're going on the wagon."

I shoved him under again and held him there until I figured he was dangerously close to drowning. The struggling had left him. I hauled his head up and waded to the shore with a firm grip on his shirt and his neck. I dropped the upper half of him on the bank and left the rest of him in the water. In a few seconds, he began coughing the water out of his throat and lungs. Michael started to bend over to tend to him.

I grabbed Michael firmly by the shoulder and looked him hard in the eye.

"Not one more drop for him."

Michael nodded.

"And when he gets his wits about him again, you tell him if there's a next time for this – I'll kill him."

I was almost as soaked as Harvey was. I took three sloppy steps to where Ted stood looking on.

"Are you all right," I asked him.

Despite all that had happened, he grinned back at me.

"Sure," he replied.

Hubert and Winston stood quietly, offering no expression, as I squished by in my soggy boots. But old Solomon smiled and slapped me on the back. I went to the cabin to get into some dry clothes, saying aside to him, "This huntin' excursion is turning out to be a whole lot more entertaining than I imagined it would be."

On the upper slope of the mountain, the wind was picking up. Tom was too sotted with apprehension and a myriad of emotions to notice it much, but Cyril was beginning to become very concerned about the turn in the weather. It was dark now, absolutely dark.

Cyril stopped, turned to Tom and spoke in a loud voice to be heard above the wind.

"We are near the spot where Homer shot his moose. We have to leave the trail now. It's near three-quarters of a mile yet to where we needs to go. It would be good if we could get there and back down at least this far before the storm hits. Stay close behind me. Ya sing out now, if ya falls. I may not hear in this wind, if ya don't."

With that pronouncement, he started off. Tom followed closely, stumbling at times, no more than two or three steps behind him. How in the world could he possibly see, or know at all, where he was going, Tom thought. But forge ahead they did, across the same expanse where a careless young bull moose had trotted towards his rendezvous with death a mere day and a half earlier.

Tom slipped and went down. He cracked his shin on a rock, but he did not call out or hesitate. He jumped back to his feet and stepped hurriedly in the direction of the sound of Cyril's movement. The going was really hard here, almost dangerously wicked. There was no one but himself to blame for being there though. He had asked for it. Another man would have suffered through the night and waited until the next morning to climb the mountain, but not him. He had to know, right now. The closer they came to the summit, the more he had to know, and the more he worried about what he would learn. He worried so much that he became frightened. The dangers of the mountain did not frighten him, but the prospect of what he might hear when he made the call was beginning to scare the hell out of him.

The wind buffeted them while they waded through the dense tangle of knee-high vegetation where they crossed over a rocky knob. They dropped over the other side of it and across a couple hundred yards of bog, before they began climbing through a tangle of gnarled spruce. The trees cut the wind, but their constant swaying and whipping made for befuddling motion in the darkness. The whistling of the wind through the tree tops and branches drowned the sound of all else. Tom flailed about in the whipping branches, desperately seeking some sound or movement from Cyril. Very suddenly, it occurred to him that Cyril was nowhere around him. He turned frantically, slipped and fell. It was no time to be proud, he thought. He began yelling, "Cyril! . . . Cyril!"

"Tommy."

Tom strained to hear the voice.

"Tommy, I'm standing still. Can you come to me?"

Tom heard the voice. It was faint, but he heard it. He yelled back, at the top of his lungs.

"I hear you, Cyril! I'm coming!"

He regained his feet and struggled up the slope.

"Cyril."

"Tommy."

The voice was much closer now. Tom climbed several more steps.

"Cyril."

"Tommy."

The voice came from only a few feet away this time. Tom took a couple more steps, then encountered Cyril immediately in front of him.

"Are ya all right, Tommy?"

"I'm okay. I just got lost from you," Tom yelled above the wind.

"Here," Cyril yelled. "Ya hang on to the handle of me ax. I hang onto the other end and we don't get separated."

Tom grabbed the ax handle and they started off again.

Wrestling through the spruce, they finally stepped out into the open, onto a slippery, short-grass covered slope. After a few yards, they climbed above the protective break of the trees, and the wind, blowing ever harder, began to pummel them.

Tom came to a very abrupt stop when he bumped solidly against Cyril's back.

"Don't move Tommy," Cyril yelled, over the sound of the wind.

A second later, Cyril clicked on his flashlight. Tom nearly jumped out of his skin. The light shone into nothingness. Cyril shined the light down to reveal that they were literally standing at the edge of a precipitous drop-off.

"Hmph," Cyril said. "I thought that's where we might be."

Tom swallowed hard as he looked down at the reflection of the light off the dark, foreboding water of one of the bottomless bathtubs, some thirty feet or more below then.

"It's only about fifty yards to the top. I think we'll use the light the rest of the way."

"Good – good idea," Tom replied.

They stepped back, away from the hazardous precipice and scrambled the rest of the way up the steep slope. There was a very large rock, about ten feet high, with bushes to the left of it. Cyril led Tom to the right, around to the leeward side of the rock. When they were suitably sheltered from the wind, Cyril turned and shined the light onto Tom's chest.

"I hold the light so you can see the numbers on the phone."

Tom pulled the cell phone from his coat pocket and hesitated. *This was it,* he thought. He looked at Cyril.

"Whatever the news is, you can survive it," Cyril said. "You made it all the way up here in the dark. You're a good and strong man."

Tom nodded. He turned the phone toward the light. His hands began to tremble. With all the fear and apprehension in the world, he punched the numbers. Placing the phone to his ear, he was relieved to hear the tone of it making the appropriate connection and ringing. One ring and nothing. He pressed the phone tight to his ear to hear over the wail of the wind. The second ring seemed to last an eternity. Then came the familiar sound of his daughter's voice.

"Hello."

"Jennifer?"

"Daddy?"

Tom hesitated, loath to ask the simple question that he had to ask.

"Jennifer, is your mother there? Is she all right?"

"Yes," she replied.

Suddenly, he was not standing on a windswept mountain top a thousand miles away. He was mentally transported to the warm embrace of his home, where his wife of twenty years was already standing beside her daughter and receiving the phone from her.

"Tom," she said in a trembling voice.

"Oh, Barbara," Tom sighed.

They both began to weep.

Cyril set the light down on a rock and stepped away. He managed to strike a match in his hat and lit his last cigarette.

Ted and I were sitting in the kitchen. It was nearly two o'clock in the morning. Hubert, Winston and Sol had gone to bed. We looked out the open door at the steady drizzle driven at an angle by the wind.

"It's gotta be one miserable son-of-a-bitch up on the mountain," I said.

"That's got to be the understatement of the year," Ted replied. I wish they'd get back. This is starting to worry me."

A couple minutes later, Cyril came through the door.

"You made it back alive," I said, in a congratulatory manner.

"Yayes."

"Where's Tom?" Ted asked.

"He went to the cabin," Cyril said, motioning with his hand as he took off his rain coat. Ted got up and rushed out the door.

"What's the report?" I asked.

"His wife is okay. Harvey's too."

"Well, flop on down. Sol left some chow for you. I'll fish it out of the oven."

Over at the cabin, Ted stepped through the door just after Tom. Michael stood up as they stepped inside. Harvey was sitting pathetically beside the stove with a bandage on the side of his face. Tom looked at him in an uneasy manner as he took off his rain gear and hung it on a nail near the door.

"Well?" Ted asked.

"Barbara's all right," Tom said. "She's pretty shaken, but all right." He looked at Harvey. "Cheryl's okay too. She had a narrow escape. She was barely out of the building before it collapsed."

Harvey looked up at him and nodded at the news of his wife. He was still wheezing and coughing.

"What the hell happened here?" Tom asked.

"That big logger almost drowned him in the lake," Michael said.

"When you consider that he pulled a gun on him and shot a hole through the wall almost killing me, I'd say Homer let him off pretty easy," Ted said, in a forceful, annoyed voice. He looked at Harvey with contempt. "If I see you even touch a gun, for the rest of this trip, I'll shoot you myself . . . " He turned to Tom. "I'm damn glad your wife's okay. There's some food for you over in the kitchen. I've had enough fun and games for one day, I'm going to bed."

Tom handed the cell phone back to Michael.

"Thanks," he said. "Michael, your friend Harold Johnson is dead. He was in the Trade Center evacuating the injured when it collapsed. I suspect we have all lost other friends as well. There's just so many unaccounted for, and so much that isn't known yet."

Michael nodded, but said nothing.

Then Tom looked back at Harvey.

"I told Barbara to tell Cheryl you turned your ankle and couldn't make the climb to call her."

"Thanks, buddy," Harvey replied.

"I didn't do it for you. I did it for her."

Harvey looked up at him. Tom gave him a hard look.

"When we get out of here, I don't ever want to see you again."

Harvey hung his head. Tom turned and walked out the door.

Cyril had just finished eating and stepped into the back room when Tom came into the kitchen.

"I heard the news – must be a hell of a relief," I said.

"Yes, it really is."

I looked at him. He was cold, wet, bruised, and exhausted. Still, he was smiling. Despite the ordeal, he felt alive again.

"Well, there's some warm chow here for you. You might as well flop on down and have at it."

"Thanks. I'm hungry enough now."

He sat down and started eating. Cyril came walking through in his underwear, with a towel over his shoulder.

"I'm off to the shower and then to bed," he said, stepping out the door.

"He's one of the most amazing men I've ever seen," Tom said. "As dark as it is out there, I don't know how we got up there and back. Even though I did it, it will always be a mystery to me."

"He's got blue eyes," I said. "Some of us blue-eyed people see better in the dark than you brown-eyed people."

"I don't know. I think he's like Luke Skywalker. I think the force is with him."

I smiled.

"It could be you're right."

After he had eaten some more, he paused.

"I can't believe – after all that happened – how incredibly lucky I am to have my wife and children unscathed."

"I doubt luck had anything to do with it. And if she worked in the World Trade Center, she can't be completely unscathed."

"Oh sure, her office is completely gone, and the company may be devastated, but she's okay. That's all that really matters to me."

"I see what you mean," I said. "About fifteen years ago, my house burned down. All the wife and I had was the clothes on our back. It knocked me for quite a loop. But after a while, I came to realize that anything that hard work or money can replace is not really a grave loss. The only thing that can't be replaced in some fashion is living beings."

"That's right. Nothing else really matters."

He resumed eating.

"Get you some more of that roast?" I offered.

"No. No thanks, this is fine."

"Cyril told me how the second plane crashed just a floor above your wife's office. When it crashed she yelled for everyone to just drop everything and head for the stairwell."

"Yeah. They were all out of the building and a safe distance away only a few minutes before the whole thing collapsed. It was close."

"She did the right thing then, at the right time, and that's why she's still alive."

"Yeah, I guess."

I reached and poured some water in his glass.

"Thanks."

"You know, I was thinking a while ago about the dog we had when I was a kid on the farm."

Tom looked at me as he chewed.

"He was a little Manchester terrier, weighed about eight pounds. Was so ungodly vicious he was actually comical. One day he chased a tomcat across the road right in front of a milk truck. Now my brothers and I dearly loved that dog. I can still remember how my little brother and I stood there, completely helpless, and watched that thirty-five tons of truck about to squash old Bruiser like a bug and – "

"Bruiser?"

"Yeah, great name for a little dinky dog, huh? . . . Anyway, we were sure the dog was going to die. But, the little dude was smart, and he had lightning fast reflexes. In a split second, he flattened himself against the ground and the truck passed right over him and never touched him . . ."

Tom looked at me and I continued.

"I've got to say, in all my life since that day, I never cringed like that until this evening when I saw you get the news about the attack . . . By God, I'm just awful glad I didn't have to see you get squashed."

He looked at me, with a broad smile.

"I'm just awful glad too."

He finished eating and I took his dishes to the sink. After a couple minutes, he asked, "So whatever happened to the little dog?"

"Oh, he led a long and hazardous life. Had

innumerable brushes with death. But, he lived to be over fourteen years old – a pretty ripe old age for a dog. One day he had a stroke, keeled over and died . . . The point is, he was just a little dinky dog, in a world where absolutely everything was bigger and more powerful than he was, but he survived by being a fighter, and by doing exactly the right thing at exactly the right time."

Tom took a drink from his glass and nodded a little. I could see he was getting my drift.

"It was one rough son-of-a-bitch today. But your wife and you both did the right thing at the right time, and you're going to be all right because of it."

CHAPTER SIX

The next day, it was as if the entire camp had a hangover. The rude sound of the generator was not heard, and no one stirred until a couple hours after sunrise. Harvey closed the door and hid out in the little 7 x 9 foot room where he and Michael bunked. He only emerged to take care of necessary bodily functions, and he did that on the sly while the rest of us were occupied with breakfast.

Ted and Winston went off hunting as though nothing had happened. Michael had apparently lost all interest in shooting a moose, even though I offered him the use of my rifle. It was very evident that his only interest was in getting out of the camp and back to New York as soon as possible.

It was nearly noon when we heard the approach of the single-engine Cessna float plane. The clouds had hung low over the mountains all morning, but had parted to allow a little sunshine to filter through an hour before. Angus was taking advantage of the window of flying opportunity. I was standing on the porch in front of the kitchen with Tom and Michael.

Cyril came out of the kitchen and yelled to Hubert, who had walked out onto the dock to look at the plane.

"Is it the skipper?"

"Yes," Hubert called back. "He's coming in."

"It would be good," Cyril said, "if we didn't mention the bullet hole in the wall to the skipper. He's a by-the-book feller and he'll have the police here for a big investigation."

"Agreed," Tom said. Michael nodded in agreement.

"Unless you really wants an investigation, Homer?"

"No," I replied. "What I'd like to see, more than anything else, is Harvey on that plane and gone."

That was a good plan as far as everyone was concerned, especially Harvey. Cyril dashed off to the cabin. By the expression on his face, it was quite evident that he was about to have a short, not very sweet talk with Harvey.

The plane set down on the lake and motored in toward the dock. Cyril came out of the cabin and shut the door behind him. He looked at us, raised his eyebrows and shook his head once, then walked down to the dock. As he and Hubert were securing the plane to the dock, Michael stepped off the porch and went down to meet Angus. Angus got out of the cockpit, they had a short conversation, and Michael went trotting off to the cabin.

"Well, it looks like your friends are leaving you," I said.

"Friend," Tom replied, looking at me.

I knew exactly what he meant.

Angus came walking up to the porch. He was a fine gentleman who was a very fit and young looking seventy years old. He extended his hand to Tom.

"You got the news about what happened in New York, I understand. Your family's all right?"

"Yes. I'm one of the lucky ones. They're all right."

"I'm taking these two friends of yours out now. They're apparently pretty anxious to get back home. It will be the last flight out today, though. There's more rough weather coming in from the coast already. Doesn't sound too good for tomorrow either."

"Whenever you can get back safely to fly me out will be soon enough," Tom said. "My family is safe. There's no emergency."

"What about you?"

Angus turned to me.

"Don't worry about me," I replied. "These other fellows have got more pressing business at home than I do."

"Good enough," Angus said. He turned and went down to the storage building where Hubert and Cyril were stowing away the things he had brought in.

Three minutes later, the door to the cabin opened and Harvey emerged. He didn't speak to anyone or even cast a glance around. He looked straight ahead and made a beeline for the plane with a bag in either hand. Cyril went after him to get him loaded into the aircraft. Michael emerged next, wrestling with his luggage. Hubert stepped up and grabbed his bags. Tom and I stepped over to say our goodbyes.

"I'm sorry Tom," Michael said. "I didn't even ask if you wanted to be on this plane. It was thoughtless of me."

"No," Tom said, "you're a paramedic. They need you back home. You go, and don't feel guilty about it. Have a safe trip."

They shook hands and Michael turned to me.

"I'm sorry I destroyed your rifle," I said.

"It's okay. Harvey gave me his," he said with a smile, holding up the fancy leather rifle case. "There's no hard feelings. You did what you had to do."

"You're a good man, Michael, " I said.

We shook hands, and he headed for the plane. He loaded up, and Hubert and Cyril shoved the aircraft away from the dock. Angus started the engine and they motored away.

Tom and I stood on the porch and watched them go.

"That Griffin & Howe Mauser of Harvey's has got to be worth what – eight or nine times what that old Remington of Michael's was."

"Yeah," Tom mused. "Maybe Harvey has some semblance of a conscience after all."

Harvey had been an antagonistic presence in the camp. With him gone, spirits lifted and good humor was restored. Tom surely had some deep concern with his wife's troubles, however, his outward demeanor returned to a pleasant, affable manner. He appeared to resume enjoying himself and making the very best of his captivity in the wilderness.

We were sitting on the porch in the afternoon, feeding the jays some scraps of bread. Cyril came out of the kitchen with a fishing rod.

"We has this old rod and reel, if ya fellers care to try your hand at fishing. The fishin', she's not so good in the lake, but who knows – maybe you get lucky and snags a sheet of that plywood, ay."

He made a lewd gesture with the rod and we all laughed at his running joke. He stepped back into the kitchen.

"Ain't that right Sol, old boy. To hell with them condoms – I wants to buy the sheet of plywood, ay?"

Tom finally stopped laughing and turned to me.

"You want to give it a try?"

"No, I can't catch fish," I replied. "You try it, and I'll watch."

Tom grabbed the rod from where Cyril had leaned it and we headed for the lake.

"You can't catch fish, huh?" He said, as we walked out onto the dock.

"No, it's like my hands exude fish repellent or something. I once stood knee deep in the Kenai River in Alaska for a day and a half, with salmon and trout in the water all around me and never caught a thing. Everybody around me was crankin' 'em in right and left... The Little Guy even jumped in and caught this huge king salmon," I said, holding out my hands.

"The Little Guy?"

"That was my dog."

He chuckled a little.

"You surely have interesting names for your dogs. What was that one you were telling me about last night? Bruiser?"

"Yeah," I said. "Well, the Little Guy was about the size of a young grizzly. And about twice as ornery."

Tom made a cast with the rod.

"You know, this is the first time I've had a line in the water since I was in high school," he said.

He turned the crank on the reel and retrieved the spinner bait, like he had been doing it all his life. It was obvious he had been a fisherman once, in his youth. It was also obvious that he thought it had been too long since he had fished.

"I have a sense," he said, "that you have had some interesting adventures... I envy that a little."

"Well, don't envy it too much. I expect I have done a few things that most folks would consider out of the ordinary. Don't get me wrong, I wouldn't trade my memories for anything, but quite often the telling about them is a whole lot more interesting than actually living them."

He took another cast.

"I think the last couple days have probably been some of the most interesting I've had lately," I said. "Who knows, maybe the next book I write will be about your and Cyril's heroic climb to the top of the mountain last night."

Tom looked at me and laughed a little.

"It wasn't that big of a deal."

"I don't know. It strikes me, in a major way, as something an ordinary man wouldn't have had the guts to do. You see, the difference between a serious writer – or at least a serious observer, and everybody else is that we can see the drama in life when it happens. Yesterday is going to go down as one of the biggest days in modern history. The question for the next generation is not going to be 'Where were you when Kennedy was assassinated?' It's going to be, 'Where were you on September eleventh, 2001?' "

"I see where you're coming from," he said. "So you'll write this whole experience down, and years from now, when I'm bouncing a grandchild on my knee, and he or she asks, 'Where were you on that fateful day, Granddaddy?' I'll pull down your book and say, 'Why right there, dear, on the pages of this book.' "

"There you go."

We laughed a little, and stared out over the soothing, peaceful water of the lake. It was a muse – just a foolish laugh – the kind countless numbers of men, throughout history, had no doubt had in the calm after the storms in their lives. Healing and reflection are for the living. A big piece of Tom Coach's psyche lived in a tormented sphere a thousand miles away. Thousands of souls around him were lost forever, but he was still alive.

CHAPTER SEVEN

A heavy mist was falling the next morning. Nevertheless, Ted and Winston were up early. They donned their rain gear after breakfast and headed off in search of a moose.

A while later, I was sitting in the outhouse, with my pants below my knees. The smell was bad, even for a privy, so I had left the door wide open. Suddenly, I heard something outside. I looked up just in time to see a big cow moose step up. She swung her head to the side and stuck her nose in the doorway, until it was no more than two feet from my face. It was literally a case of being caught with my pants down. I was cornered and at the mercy of an eight-hundred pound beast with a reputation for occasional fits of ill temper. Every story I had ever heard about a moose stomping someone to death raced through my mind. Before I could react in any way, and to my immense relief, she pulled her nose out of my face and continued on her way. A big calf came along right behind her and merely glanced at me as he stepped past.

Hubert had been standing in the doorway of the kitchen and hastily summoned the other men to witness the close encounter. They all stood on the porch and watched as the cow and calf merely sauntered through the camp, and proceeded down the lake shore. When I emerged from the outhouse, I was met with hoots and laughter.

"It's a good thing ya already had your pants down, ay Homer?" Cyril yelled.

"Indeed it was," I replied. "That's what I call a real motivational moment. Everything but breakfast just left me."

The joke was on me in a major way and we all had a good laugh over it.

I was standing on the dock after lunch when Tom came walking down from the cabin. The drizzle had relented a short while earlier. I was scanning the sky to determine what the weather held in store for us for the rest of the day.

"It's not going to clear up enough for flying today," I said, as Tom stepped out on the dock.

"Are you sure? I thought maybe it was starting to clear up."

"You see that raven flying over the lake?"

"Yes."

"You can tell by the way he's flying that it will be raining again in two or three hours."

Tom strained to look at the raven.

"I'll have to take your word for it," he said. "I was going to take a walk down to the end of the lake to see the rapids, where the river drains out. Do you want to come?"

"I suppose. Beats hell out of sittin' in the shitter waitin' for another moose to walk by."

We walked down the rocky shoreline the half mile to the rapids at the lower end of the lake. After climbing over and around the big rocks on the river bank, we sat down on a flat rock beside the fast, rushing, white water. After we had sat for a couple minutes, Tom spoke.

"Look at how beautiful this place is," he said. "Just look at it. The way the water flows over these rocks, it even sounds beautiful . . . I'd like to believe that God made this place, just so guys like us could sit here, on an afternoon like this, and be awed by it. It's hard though. After Tuesday, it's really hard. Times like this can really shake your faith. How could God let this happen?"

I looked at him, a little surprised by the degree of openness. He had caught me a bit off guard.

"Oh, I don't think we can lay this one off on a failure of God."

"Are you a God-fearing man, Homer?"

"Well, I don't think you could exactly call me God-fearing. I know that God exists. That's probably a pretty odd thing for someone who's not a Christian to say, but I spoke with him once, so I know that he exists. How about you?"

"I don't know. I don't know what to think. I don't know if I ever really did know."

We sat quietly for a moment. I didn't quite know what to say on the matter, but it seemed that he desperately needed for someone to say something.

"I think God is like everyone else," I said. "He has a limited amount of energy to expend. He can perform miracles sometimes – he just can't do it constantly, non-stop, all the time."

Tom thought about it. Then slowly, he replied.

"I suppose you're right. If he took care of us all the time, what would be the sense of it all? What responsibility would we have?"

"Exactly. Personally, I've never prayed to God, never asked him for anything. I prefer to put my faith in the genius and industry of men. I think we should be responsible for ourselves."

Tom never moved his gaze from the rushing water. He leaned forward with his elbows on his knees.

"Have we been that careless? Has all this happened because we were that irresponsible?" He asked.

"Yeah. Yeah, I think so . . .You know, when I think of God, I think of the question posed by Joan Osborne's song 'What if God was one of us?' I think he probably started out that way – probably a man with a broken heart, eons ago – maybe in a world far away. I feel for him. I worry for him. I think of him carrying on against insanely impossible odds, through all these eons, watching mankind make the same mistakes over and over and over again. I just can't begin to imagine how utterly depressing that must be. Now mankind has let things slide to the point that there are actual demons afoot in these times. I think even God needs all the help he can get."

"As recently as just a couple days ago, I would have listened to you say that and I would have thought you were speaking in metaphor, or maybe even that you were nuts. Now I'm not so sure."

"That's because you've had a rude education these past couple days – an abrupt awakening. And you're level headed enough to want to find the right answers, not just fly off deeper into some prejudicial, pre-conceived tangent like old Harvey." I paused and thought for a moment. "If you want the right answers, I suppose, in a way you can talk about religion. I think what we're up against probably cuts to the basic elements of most people's religion. What is the Bible really, but mostly the history of the struggles of a certain people – stories about how their rulers either succumbed or rose above strife and evil. Well here we are right in the middle of a whole chapter of our own in the monumental struggle between good and evil . . . What is the first thing they teach you in Sunday school? You learn that the way the devil succeeds is by deceiving people. Time and time again, he rules over the masses by deceiving their ministers and rulers. The failure people have with their religion in these times is that they just can't seem to apply this basic lesson to real, everyday life. Are our rulers good men who are determined to defeat evil, or are they purveyors or victims of deception? It's obvious to me that it's the latter. We didn't arrive at the straits we're in by accident. We were slowly, intentionally led here."

Tom gave no indication of having any response, so I continued.

"If you really want to get down to it, I think this may go all the way back, even beyond biblical time . . . Are you familiar with the Sumerian texts?"

"Just that it's the oldest known writing."

"That's right. Among other things, the chronicles talk about a pair of kings, two brothers actually, Enki and Enlil. You know these guys were members of the Anunnaki, a race said to have come down from the heavens. I suppose they were, in reality, some space aliens. They were supposed to be a race of giants, who lived hundreds of years. Anyway, they were in conflict about what to do with us mere humans. Enki wanted to bring enlightenment to humanity – get us up to speed with them, so we could all be equals. He saw a vast, very desirable potential for humans. But ol' Enlil, he had an entirely different view. He saw humans as a second-class species. His only interest was in keeping us under his thumb, stupid and compliant, only useful as sex objects and slaves . . . Given the course of the thousands of years of history which has transpired since those forty-seven cuneiform tablets were written, I'd say they're probably an accurate chronicle

". . . And – that in a nutshell is where we still are today."

"You're saying, what? That there's a ruling elite who regards us as second-class beings, who only exist to serve them?"

"Yeah," I said. "That's pretty much it. Occasionally one of the arrogant bastards will even shoot off his mouth and admit as much – like ol' David Rockefeller a while back. He said flat out, 'yes there is a powerful conspiracy steering humanity behind the scenes, and he was proud to be an influential part of it.' Then he was talking about some trade agreement, and some other specific things they'd pulled off, and said 'it was about time we finally got to this point, because they, and this is proof, if there ever was proof, that there really is a they – that they had been working for five hundred years to get to this point.' "

"Wow, he really said that?"

"Yeah."

"Where . . . where did you get this?"

"Oh, it wasn't in any obscure journal. It was in USA Today not too long ago."

"Wow. I mean, wow. He actually said that."

"Yeah. Of course it wasn't mentioned anywhere else. Statements like that may be intentionally ignored, but for anyone who is really paying attention, you don't forget it. It's revealing. It's confirmation of a great many things. Is it any wonder that we are now dealing with Islamic terrorists? If we had pursued the Gulf War just one more day we would have taken down Saddam Hussein. But no, George Bush, Sr. pulled the plug. Why? So that a dozen years down the road, the conspiratorial bastards he was in cahoots with would have an excuse for war. Clinton was a part of the same scheme. He did everything he could to fan the flame of Arab hatred and resentment – sent in the military on half-baked missions – bombed the aspirin factory in the Sudan, that sort of thing. For forty years, we've turned a blind eye to a global, one world government cabal financing and encouraging terrorists. If you really get down to it, Islamic fundamentalism is merely a façade. The truth is that the entire terror network is a charade, a tool to make us all fearful, to bludgeon us into submission with."

Tom finally interrupted me.

"Is that what this is about – spreading fear, so we will all fall in line behind their political agenda?"

I paused again for a moment. "If you want answers, if you really want to know what's going on, you have to look at the really big picture and you have to be objective. You gotta deal in cold, hard facts. You can't let your judgment be clouded by preconceived notions or blind allegiance to a political party, or pressure or the attitudes of your friends and associates."

"I understand what you mean," Tom said. "It's like Michael and Harvey being dyed-in-wool Democrats and automatically swallowing the party line, no matter what. They put too much trust in an institution which may have an agenda all its own."

"That's right. To be honest, I fell into the same trap for a few years when I was younger with the Republicans. Eventually, I came to see that George Washington was right when he said that political parties would be the ruination of the country . . . He was right about other things, too. He saw, way back then, that there was a conspiratorial group of the wealthy elite to whom the formation of the new republic was anathema. He wrote several pieces expressing fear about what they might do to destroy the new government. Personally, I think the U.S. Constitution laid out the best form of government yet conceived by man; far from perfect, mind you – but you can't reform something by merely tearing it down. Ya gotta have something better to replace it with. And try as I might, I just can't think of anything feasible which strikes me as better. Unfortunately, we haven't been much ruled by that esteemed document in our lifetime. For nearly ninety years, the American people have carelessly surrendered freedom to the government. The power of the government has grown incrementally until it's gotten to the point that it's run amok. At the same time, we've carelessly allowed secret societies, and what can best be called a very sophisticated, very organized criminal network to proliferate and grow in influence, until they've largely seized control of our all-powerful government. And now they've got us by the ass."

I was starting to preach and get too heavy handed, I thought. I was getting carried away and approaching the point where people usually started to tune me out. However, Tom had had the kind of shock in his life that made a man sit up and take notice. He was searching his soul over just these very issues.

He nodded his head slowly. It made sense to him. He just hadn't taken the time to think about it before.

"That's what Bush Senior was really alluding to with all his speeches about a *New World Order* – global government," Tom said.

"That's right. It had been in the works for many years. He just started coming out of the closet with it."

"So what do we do? How do we defeat them?"

I did not immediately respond to him. I couldn't. The fact was that deep down I realized that the hour was probably too late to do anything about it. The evil elite was going to have its way with the common people no matter what we did now. At the very least, they were going to drag mankind through years of war and cataclysm. But I was by nature a fighter. No matter how realistic, or pessimistic my assessment was, I would not go softly into that dark night.

"It ain't gonna be easy," I said, finally. "We're gonna have to educate a lot of people before it's too late. The only thing a few obnoxious, ranting rednecks like me, working alone, can accomplish is getting ourselves shot or thrown in prison. Somehow, we've got to get a significant portion of the population to stop being sheep."

"I guess you're right. I've been a failure. I'm a teacher. I've been too ignorant to teach anyone anything."

"I didn't mean it that way," I said.

"You know, you remind me a little of my uncle. He still lives in Vermont, where I grew up. He says New York is nothing but a city full of sheep. I remember hearing him say once that there were three kinds of people in the world: There was the majority, who were sheep, and then there were wolves, and then there were a few guard dogs . . . He always condemned my father, his brother, . . . and me, as being sheep."

I looked at him with all the empathy I could muster.

"I guess he was right. I've lived my life like a sheep."

I sighed and looked away.

"How did you get to be a guard dog?" He asked.

"Oh . . . I guess for me it was natural, genetic, in a way. I was born a pup, not a lamb. I've been a guard dog all of my life."

We sat quietly for a moment, watching the swift water flow by. Finally, Tom spoke again.

"I know what you said about the objective truth – it's true. Before we leave here, I'd like to know about where you get your information. I don't expect you to divulge the names of your intelligence sources, but if you could give me a list of publications you read, or books, I would appreciate it. It has become evident that I'm far too ignorant of what's going on. If the last few days have shown me anything, it is that there are people out there who can harm me and my family, and I need to know more about them . . . I think you are absolutely correct concerning what you said about defining moments. For you, and guys like you, it was the massacre at Waco, and the day the senate failed to remove Clinton from office. For most of the rest of us, the defining moment we're going to remember the rest of our lives is going to be September eleven, 2001. Maybe I haven't been paying enough attention to what's going on, but this – this is something that's going to shape the rest of my life."

"Yeah," I sighed. "I expect it will . . . You know, I fault myself – and others, for how we got to this point. Our own failures contributed to us getting to where we are now."

"How so?"

"Ya remember where you were when John Kennedy was shot?"

"Just barely. I was in the second grade."

"Yeah? Me – I remember it vividly. I was sitting in Mrs. Anna Farr's fourth grade class in Buffalo, Indiana . . . in alphabetical order, behind a tall, pretty girl named Cathy Roberts. The janitor was a quiet, white-haired old dude named Ed Grass. Mr. Grass pecked on the door that afternoon and stuck his head into the classroom. Mrs. Farr went to see what was up and they spoke quietly in the hall for a minute. I remember that woman well. She was a good lookin' old red-haired dame . . . had a hell of a temper, was a fearsome disciplinarian . . . but, altogether, a fine woman . . . When she came back into the classroom she went straight to her old wooden desk, at the front of the room and sat down. You could've heard a pin drop. We all sat there and we knew something really awful had happened. She took off her glasses and just stared into space. I looked at her face and it was just like the life had all gone out of her. She regained just enough composure to say to us 'President Kennedy has just been shot and killed'. Then she wept . . . Long as I live, I'll never forget how that woman looked that afternoon."

I glanced at Tom, and he was looking straight at me. It was apparently evident that even after all the years which had passed, it still pained me just to recount it.

"I remember the next day, my father coming in after feedin' some hogs and listening to the news on the radio as he had some lunch. After a while, he said to my Aunt Evelyn, 'They caught that guy, Oswald, just a little too fast and easy. There's something damned suspicious goin' on here'. He was just a farmer, a couple years older than I am right now, but the situation didn't pass the smell test with him. I think a majority of the people knew that the Warren Report was nothing but bullshit."

"Having Allen Dulles on the Warren Commission, after Kennedy was doing everything he could to fire him, and dismantle the CIA was the tip-off for my dad and my uncle that it was all just a cover-up. Do you think the CIA killed Kennedy?"

"Yes, yes I do. Kennedy was a good man. He was trying to enact major changes that the New World Order conspiracy knew would put a crimp to their plans. Killing him was nothing less than a coup. A coup which considerably altered the direction the country would take. If JFK had lived, and had some success, we wouldn't be in the straits we're in now . . . You're right. He saw he CIA as a dangerous, rouge organization which was accountable to no one, certainly not to him, congress, or the American people and he was going to fire Dulles and, as he said it, 'Tear it to a thousand pieces and scatter it to the wind'. "

"So they killed him, before he could get it done."

"Yep. That, and he was going to end our involvement in Viet Nam. And abolish the Federal Reserve and print honest money. Contrary to what most people believe, the Fed is not a government entity. It's a private banking cartel, which functions as a thinly-veiled crime syndicate. They've been suckin' the life blood out of the country for nearly ninety years now, to enrich themselves, and I've got a feeling their depredations are gonna get a whole lot worse."

"You may be right," Tom said. "Where does that leave us now, do you think?"

"Well, I guess I started talking about JFK to make a point. If we dial ahead thirty years after Kennedy was whacked, we get to the point where I had the last substantial conversation with my father. Looking back, I think the old man knew he wasn't gonna be around a whole lot longer, so he got a little serious. It was October of 1992, and he figured it didn't much matter who got elected, whether it was Bush senior or Clinton, the country was headed in a bad direction . . . Said he faulted himself, in a way. He said it had taken him some years to sort it all out, but he realized then that Kennedy being assassinated was when the dark forces really started to gain control. He said every old farmer, like him, should have taken their shotguns and marched on Washington back then; said we were all going to pay a heavy price for their failure to do it then . . . It was a few months later, after the old man had died, and after the bastards had murdered and torched the Davidians at Waco, that I realized the old man was right . . . Our father's generation failed to act after the Kennedys were shot, and our generation failed to come to the aid of the Davidians – and ourselves. A couple million of us should have armed ourselves to the teeth, jumped into our pickup trucks, drove to Waco and had it out with this rotten government right there...But we didn't. Where we are now is a direct consequence of the compounding failures of generations of us. Every time evil succeeds it gains power. They refine and perfect the art of telling the big lie and getting away with it."

"Yeeeaaah," Tom sighed. "I understand what you're saying. Nobody wants to accept the responsibility, but the burden is there all the same... So, aside from everything else, why do you think the government murdered the Davidians?"

"Well... I know a guy who says he knows why. And I expect he's right. Do you know who Eugene Hassenfoos is?"

"No. No I don't."

"Well, he's another fellow from Wisconsin. He and I have a mutual friend. You see, Ol' Hass, as they call him, was the lone survivor of a plane crash in Nicaragua about twenty years back. The story that he was forced to tell was the beginning of what came to be known as the Iran Contra Scandal."

"Now I remember. Wow, you know some interesting people."

"Yeah, I guess," I said. "Now anybody who knows anything, knows that the CIA is the biggest drug running cartel in the world."

"I've heard that. They say that's how they finance a lot of their operations."

"That's basically accurate. You see, they bring drugs into the country from Latin America and they run guns back. That's where the Davidians come in.

It's pretty common knowledge that the Davidians bought an awful lot of gun parts and assembled a lot of guns, mostly AR-15's. What's not generally known is just where all those guns went."

"Let me guess – the CIA was buying them to run them to the drug cartels in South America."

"You got the picture. Well, Bush senior and Clinton were both into it up to their eyeballs –

"Wait. Bill Clinton and George Bush in cahoots?"

"Oh yeah, they're like – best buddies."

"No way."

"Way."

"So, all the political animosity is – what – just theater."

"Exactly, just an integral part of the big lie . . . Anyway, somebody was getting nervous that the relationship between the Davidians and the CIA was going to become public, so the plan from the very beginning was to murder all those people and burn the place down to cover their tracks."

"Wow . . . I have to say, now that you have put it to me this way, it actually makes sense now that things went down the way they did at Waco."

I chuckled a bit.

"You're starting to get the hang of this now. Give me enough time, and I could turn you into a genuinely skeptical S.O.B."

"Humpf," Tom scoffed, with a smile.

"Well, one thing is pretty obvious. I've been

bumbling through life being one unobservant, overly trusting fool."

I shifted my position slightly on the hard rock.

"Well," I said, "I can't say that I fault you, or people like you, for being unobservant. Hell, the average guy and his wife work day and night just to have something of their own after the government confiscates half of their income. You go through life trying to do the best for your wife and kids, and when you finally get a moment to sit down and relax, the last thing you want to hear is some harangue from some dickhead like me. I know I'm viewed as an extremist. Hell, I suspect even my family and friends think I'm a tad eccentric . . . I've got my own reasons for being extraordinarily vigilant . . . This terrorist attack, with all the thousands of people who have died, and all those, like yourself, who are directly affected – this is a biggee. No matter who you are or where you live, this won't be forgotten. It doesn't matter what defining moments we realize, as long as we come to the same honest, objective truth in the end."

We sat quietly for a minute and watched the water flowing by.

"Look, there's an otter," I said, pointing.

"Would you look at that."

A large otter had climbed onto a rock just above the rapids with a small fish in his mouth. We sat motionless and silent, and watched him until he slipped back into the water and disappeared. We waited for him to resurface, but he did not. Finally, Tom spoke again.

"I got the impression, by a couple remarks you made yesterday, that you think we're headed for a major war over this."

"Oh, it's not just an idle speculation. I'm quite certain of it. It has become increasingly obvious to me for several years now, that it's a part of the overall plan. It's the reason why Bush left Saddam in power back in '91 and why Clinton kowtowed to the North Koreans and sold so much military technology to the Chinese. You wait, it will start with a couple smaller scale operations in the Middle East and it will gradually escalate over a period of several years until half the world will be shooting at each other . . . The problem with war is that the real truth of what is going on is often pretty hard to sort out. Even in World War Two, when the cause seemed noble enough, we had generals who realized that the whole thing was a racket. And when it was over, we lost in a major way. Communism made gigantic gains and the United Nations, which is now poised to become the most onerous political entity of all times, was established. These days, no one seems to have a clue that the charter for the U.N. was actually written by a couple communists – before the U.S. was ever involved in the war. The U.N. was designed from the beginning to be the prime instrument for the *New World Order* elite to accomplish their goals. You've got to look at what they do, not what they claim for a mission. The U.N. may claim to be a humanitarian organization founded to quote, "save succeeding generations from the scourge of war," but in fact they have promoted and drawn out war as a means of furthering their designs for world domination. Korea, Viet Nam, Somalia – all of our U.N. sanctioned conflicts have been complete disasters."

"Yes, you're certainly right about that. The past fifty years have seen more war than any other period in history."

"The dangers of all this are pretty hard to get across to people though."

"Oh yeah," Tom said. "Especially when you get into politics. Everything you just said gets into pretty contentious territory. Personally, I avoid talking about anything political like the plague. You can find yourself in the middle of a vicious argument in a hurry. When it comes to bias, the bigotry associated with things like race and religion doesn't even begin to compare with the way some people feel about politics."

"You're sure right about that."

"One thing has become painfully obvious to me," Tom said. "Tuesday was a wake-up call. Political bias has to be, somehow, set aside. We have come to a time when people have to know and accept the truth."

"You've got that right," I said. "The sad fact is that all through history, hundreds of millions of good men have fought for despicable leaders, for causes they didn't begin to understand. Now here we are again, heading for World War Three on the course of a massive manipulation by a bunch of devious, evil fucks who don't give a damn if they kill millions of the common people to further their global government design. The tragedy is we may be on the verge of it being too late to do anything to stop it. When the barbarians are at the gate, you have to fight for survival, no matter what the original provocation was. There's gonna be war all right – a hell of a war. Every boy, like yours, who's ten years old now will be drafted into fighting in it. And even if we win the fight, we can still lose. If the New World Orderlies get their way when it comes time to negotiate peace, the way they did back in World War Two, we will have lost in a major way. People are already waving the flag and getting that old patriotic feeling all over – which is fine – it really warms the heart. But I hope to hell, when the shit hits the fan and we're in the all-out battle, that we'll be fighting for the people of the United States of America, not for the damned Council on Foreign Relations, the U.N. and the Bilderbergers."

Tom looked up from where he had been staring at his feet.

"I sure hope you're wrong about all this, but I fear you are right," he said. "I've got to hand it to you, you sure know how to paint a pretty picture."

I looked at him and smiled in response to his facetious comment.

"Yeah, and I gave you the short, sweet, sugar-coated version."

He looked at me and smiled a little.

"I wish I could laugh at that, but something tells me it's just a little too accurate to be funny. So, September eleven, 2001 was the beginning of a cataclysm," he said in a resigned manner.

"That's right. The dust may not settle on this for twenty years, but when it does, it's a certainty that, for better or worse, the world will be turning on a whole new axis."

CHAPTER EIGHT

The weather cleared the next morning, and towards noon Angus' single-engine Cessna once again descended from the sky and settled upon the peaceful water of the lake. Ted had shot his moose the previous evening and was now ready to leave. He and Tom had their luggage waiting on the dock when the plane coasted in, and was caught and secured.

I was standing where the dock met the shore with Ted and Tom. I extended my hand to Ted and said, "by God, it's sure been good knowing you."

"Same here." He shook my hand and turned to get loaded onto the plane.

"I'm glad you were here with us," Tom said, shaking my hand. "You're an interesting man to have met."

"Well, I've been called interesting enough times to know that it's not always a compliment."

We had a bit of a last laugh.

"Well, it is this time. I'm going to hit the ground

running on the other end of this flight, so I may never see you again."

"I ain't likely to ever go to New York City again," I said. "But if you ever get to Rhinelander, Wisconsin, you and yours are welcome at my house any time."

He nodded appreciatively and turned to go. I followed him part of the way out onto the dock. Cyril grabbed his hand as they ducked beneath the wing of the aircraft.

"Well, Tommy, the wife and the little ones are gonna look pretty good when ya gets home, ay?"

"Yes, to say the least."

It was quite evident that he was having a difficult time saying good-bye to Cyril.

"I don't know how I'll ever be able to repay you for what you did for me."

"Ah, it was just another walk up the hill. Maybe you come again and we hunt some more. Next time, ya brings the wife along, so we doesn't have to call her in the middle of the night."

They both smiled broadly.

"You never know," Tom replied. "I just may do that."

He turned and climbed into the plane. Hubert and Winston untied the ropes and Angus started turning the engine over.

"Just one more thing," Cyril said, leaning slightly into the plane. "When ya gets back to civilization, ya tell 'em to send us a sheet of that plywood, ay."

I couldn't tell from where I was standing, but I think Tom had a tear in his eye as he laughed.

I stood with the four Canadians and watched the plane lift off the water and disappear over the mountain.

Not much more can be said of my short acquaintance with Tom Coach except this: On rare occasion, we meet individuals in passing who leave a profound impression on us, and this he surely did.

With all flights grounded, many after being diverted, all over North America, for several days after the tragedy, thousands of passengers found themselves stranded in Newfoundland. With no room left at an inn anywhere on the island, the people of Newfoundland opened their homes to the hapless travelers, thus proving themselves to indeed be the friendliest people in the world.

The most noteworthy thing which could be said of my two-thousand mile drive home was that flags were waving absolutely everywhere. Americans, and even some Canadians, demonstrated powerfully that patriotism and defiance in the face of attack were the order of the day. Even with my trepidations for the situation, and knowing how entirely misdirected it all was, it was, nevertheless, heart-warming.

When I returned home, my ever popular and community-minded wife was in the middle of a big fund raiser for the victims of the terrorist attack. She had mobilized a small army of her high school students, and issued a very specific and personal challenge to them and the community at large. One of her more enterprising students made a giant placard which was featured on the front page of the local newspaper. It read: HELP US RAISE $15,000 SO WE CAN SHAVE MS. MACHTAN'S HEAD.

It was a pretty lofty goal for a town of nine thousand souls, very few of whom had ever seen New York City, or cared to. Nevertheless, the goal was far surpassed and before I knew it, I was watching my wife lose her hair on the television news. I was pretty accepting and had a sense of humor about her hair loss while in an awake, cognizant state, but a couple times when I absently reached over in the middle of the night and my hand settled down on a bald head, I was awakened with quite a start.

I never heard from Tom Coach again, though I wondered about him from time to time. Near Christmas, I very unexpectedly got a phone call from our guide, Cyril. He said he had received a Christmas card from Tom. It said he had bought a house near a small town in Vermont and was going to move his family there the following summer. He said he was leaving Rome and becoming a subject. And he was in training to become a guard dog. Cyril asked me what that meant? I said, simply, that it meant he was a good man, concerned about his family and society in general.

"Yayes," Cyril replied, "he's a good one, that

Tommy. He's a fellow you can always count on to do the right thing."

The End

EPILOGUE

To accept the official version of the events of September 11, 2001 is to defy logical thinking, eye witness accounts of those who were there, and all physical evidence. With hundreds of books having been written exposing the gargantuan lie, I will not add to the fine detail here, but merely point out a few of the most obvious detractions and encourage the reader to investigate further.

The most immediate and obvious aspect of the events of that day which should have tipped off any conscious observer that all was not kosher, was the purposeful destruction of the third building of the World Trade Center complex. Despite having received no irreparable damage, building number seven, I believed it was called, was brought down in a controlled demolition on the afternoon of 9/11. Like millions of other people, I have seen the video tape of Larry Silverstein, the gazillionaire owner of the World Trade Center complex, saying they made the decision to "pull" building number seven that afternoon.

Now, aside from the insurance fraud implications, one can't just make a decision to blow up a building and do it an hour or two later. It takes a crew of knowledgeable and experienced men weeks to plant charges and wire the building to get it done. The obvious question is, just exactly why was this building, where people were working and going about their business every day, wired for demolition in advance of 9/11?. . . And, since it surely was, it is no stretch of the imagination to assume that the twin towers, right next door, were also similarly charged and wired. There were a considerable number of New York City firemen who maintained that the towers were brought down in just that fashion. They could hear and feel the charges detonating in rapid succession on the floors above their heads as they fled the building. All of them didn't make it out. Those who did were told by their superiors to not talk about the purposeful demolition. Those who persisted in talking about it we told in no uncertain terms that if they valued their jobs, they would shut the hell up about it. There were several who had the balls and the righteous indignation to refuse to shut up and were in fact fired. The fact that no major news organization would give them the time of day, proves that the mainstream media is wholly owned by the cabal which pulled off this most dastardly of deeds.

Then there was the problem with the other two "planes" which crashed. Almost no one who observed or took part in cleaning up the debris at the Pentagon was convinced that it was a commercial airliner. What struck the building was either a military drone or a cruise missile. The same could be said for the crash in Pennsylvania. Whatever hit the ground there was not a commercial airliner. Author Victor Thorn lived not far from Shankesville, and was on the scene mere hours after the crash and saw right off that something was badly amiss with the official story. He wrote the definitive volume on that crash, called *Mysterious Flight 93*.

There was also a problem with the famed list and profiles of the nineteen Arab hijackers. The government claimed to have no advance warning of the attack; nevertheless, they conveniently produced a list of the supposed perpetrators, in time for the evening news, the very next day. The inconvenient truth, which has never been mentioned in the American news media, is that at least nine of these men were alive and well, and living in various parts of the world on September 12 . . . Ooops. Mohammed Atta, the supposed ring leader, was in his apartment, in Germany, and made a couple phone calls, one to his father in Egypt. Of course, he then disappeared. Either he went into hiding, or was quietly murdered to maintain the official lie. Another man was widely seen on various Arab TV outlets, smiling at the camera as he held up a newspaper with the headline of the day, thus proving that he had not committed suicide on an airliner in America.

A gravely ill and dying man named Osama bin Laden became famous as the official boogeyman for the 9/11 attack. Though he admitted to not being philosophically opposed to what had happened, he maintained he had nothing to do with it. It is worthy to note that several members of the bin Laden family were friends and business partners with the Bush family. With every last airplane, everywhere in North America grounded, and tens of thousands of travelers stranded across the continent, 28 members of the bin Laden clan were allowed to quietly board a plane and fly away from the United States of America on September 12. It was widely reported in the Arab world that Osama bin Laden died in December of 2001. There was a funeral. A lot of people attended. One would think that this would have at least rated mentioning in the American press, but it did not. The boogeyman had to live on for another decade, to justify more war.

A couple years after 9/11, a major poll showed that fully 48 percent of the American people did not believe the official version of the events of that horrible day. The criminal cabal which jerks the chain of our government manikins saw the necessity of establishing a commission to study the issue and quell the dissent. Of course, it was just like every other such "investigation" since the Warren Commission farce. Yet another distinguished pack of coyotes was appointed to investigate the disappearances of chickens from the hen house. The conclusion was forgone before the proceedings ever began. And so, one of the most damnable, destructive lies in the history of humanity persists.

"Why in the world would they do that?" comes the incredulous refrain from the terminally ignorant masses who just can't believe (no matter how much cold, hard evidence smacks them in the face) that their own government would kill three thousand of its own citizens to promote a political agenda. The answer is, it's about empire. It's about having hundreds of military bases in countries all over the world. It's about bullying the citizens of the world to their design for global domination. It's about the super rich becoming super richer, and the rest of us becoming their slaves.

In one of his speeches on the subject, when he was the president, George H.W. Bush said, with great enthusiasm, "there will be a new world order. And the people of the world, including Americans, will be dragged into it kicking and screaming if necessary." All those years ago, I remember when he uttered those words, I sat up in my easy chair, stared at the television screen and thought *what the hell is he talking about?*

We've had a considerable number of years now to see what he was talking about and it's obviously a nefarious design no good person should accept.

There are those who pronounce these "conspiracy

theories" as somehow unpatriotic, or even disrespectful of the people who perished on September 11, 2001. I have no respect for either the intellect or judgement of such people. They are the unpatriotic, and disrespectful of the dead. The dead deserve the truth to be told, and their murderers brought to justice . . . Though justice never comes easy when the criminals are the state.

ABOUT THE AUTHOR

Homer Van Meter is a writer, researcher, and investigator. He also owns a logging company in northern Wisconsin, where he lives with his wife and three dogs. *Living in Rome* is the most recent volume in a series which includes *Day of the Little Guy, 4900 Nights: A True Story of Reincarnation,* and *The Dreaming Time: Anatomy of a Cover Up.*

www.ingramcontent.com/pod-product-compliance
Lightning Source LLC
Chambersburg PA
CBHW042114100526
44587CB00025B/4051